HERE WALKS MY ENEMY

HERE WALKS MY ENEMY

The Story of Luis

Zane C. Hodges

REDENCIÓN VIVA

Box 141167
Dallas, Texas 75214

HERE WALKS MY ENEMY

Contents

The story in the following pages is true. The events and situations have been reconstructed as accurately as possible, within the limits of human memory. Many names have been changed to protect the privacy of the persons involved.

1
Highway to Peril

Luis watched the Mexican countryside roll by along the road from San Felipe, Guanajuato. From the driver's seat of his Ford economy-line 250 van, nothing looked particularly different on this trip than it had looked on any of a half-dozen trips before.

There was certainly nothing to warn him that within hours he would be staring at death down the barrel of a loaded machine gun.

The conversation inside the van proceeded in fits and spurts. Angel occupied the seat next to Luis, and Octavio the couch to Luis's rear.

"Hey, Luis, look over there!" Angel spoke up. "Those are the *aguas medicinales!* That's where people come to get cured of their rheumatism and arthritis! Remember?"

"Come on, Angel!" The exchange was in Spanish. "How is warm water going to cure rheumatism and arthritis?" *It figured,* Luis thought. *Just another of the endless cures you always heard about in Mexico.* He treated them all with the skepticism they deserved.

"But it's true!" Angel insisted. "Lots of people come down from the United States just for that."

"Well, anyway, I swam in them one time."

"You swam in the new ones over here." With a nod Angel indicated his side of the highway. "They've modernized those. But the old ones are over there. That's where all the people come to be cured."

The hot springs, called *Ojo Caliente* in Spanish, were situated in more rugged terrain than the countryside they had just left behind them. The narrow black-top road out of San Felipe had carried them some minutes before past a large dairy ranch dotted with barns and corrals full of cows. Now the landscape was more barren and the ground was largely grassless and rock-strewn. Scattered here and there were various kinds of shrubs, in particular the prickly Indian pear-trees, called *nopales*. In the background, on either side of the highway, lay the mountains. And ahead lay trouble.

It had rained for five days in San Felipe. That was not exactly the kind of weather Luis had been hoping for. He had come down alone to hunt, while Felisita and the two boys had stayed behind in Dallas. These were Feliz's people down here — her father, an aging grandmother, and numerous cousins, among whom Angel and Octavio were merely two.

Maybe the rains had washed out his hunting plans, but they had failed to dampen the simple pleasures of a visit to San Felipe. The memories from this most recent trip had already begun to enrich the agreeable associations which that city, deep in the Mexican interior, had for Luis. Warmth and hospitality, dignity and self-respect — these were the pleasing qualities of its people who, at the superficial level of material well-being, might have been called "poor."

Who, for example, could forget the sight of the *rancheros*, dressed as always in their nondescript shirts and baggy pants, coming on a Sunday morning to San Felipe's market to buy food and goods? From the surrounding countryside they came, their feet shod in sandal-like *huaraches*, the women wearing the dark-colored shawls called *rebozos*. No one moved any faster than the indispensable burros which accompanied them and which often pulled wagons in which some of the family could ride.

The market which attracted them was housed in a large building and its stalls were arranged in the shape of a gigantic U. The legs of this U ran along either side of the host structure until they curved and met along the wall farthest from the main entryways.

The sights and sounds, the tastes and smells, of this market-place loomed large in the recollections Luis had of San Felipe. Especially the tastes! Luis often moved quickly past the tables of dry goods which occupied the front portion of the open space between the legs of the U and which were cluttered with yo-yos, dolls, fans, combs, knives, mirrors, and countless other salable items. He would make his way down one line of stalls which retailed fish and meats and vegetables until he came to Pedro's oyster bar. And there he could enjoy un *cóctel de camarones!*

Pedro was another of his wife's cousins, and the *cóctel de camarones* he served up was without equal. A delicious shrimp cocktail, it was enlivened by the addition of spooned-out *aguacate*, by hot or mild *salsa* (which had the appearance of catsup), and by *tomate*, onions, and a flavoring weed known as *cilantro*. This exotic combination, which Luis preferred with mild *salsa* and no onions, was usually enjoyed with crackers, and in his view it was a treat that almost justified the entire trip to San Felipe.

The van had now reached the intersection with highway 57, where a northward turn would shortly carry them around the outskirts of the city of San Luis, Potosí. To the south the road led to Mexico City, a metropolis which teemed with a population larger than all but a handful of the world's cities. Beyond San Luis, in the direction they were heading, lay Saltillo, Monterrey, and finally Laredo. That was as far as Angel and Octavio would go, leaving Luis to travel the remaining miles to Dallas alone.

On the fringes of San Luis, Potosí, a breakfast stop at a small café refreshed the three travelers. By a kind of irony it was a *Japanese* place called El Restaurante Tokyo!

Briefly but fruitlessly Luis looked around for a can of Choco Milk. It would be easily recognized by its familiar trademark of a red-shirted Mexican cowboy, "Pancho Pantera," flexing his muscles with the energy the contents of the can supposedly provided. "Alimento, Vitaminado, Mineralizado" described the assets which Choco Milk grandly offered its users. Luis was tempted to smile when he thought of Zane, his "gringo" friend in Dallas, who would be sorely disappointed if a can of his favorite chocolate mix failed to materialize when Luis did! But there wasn't any to be had here, and soon the van was rolling up the highway, leaving the city of San Luis behind it.

The countryside had changed only slightly, with distant mountain ranges still visible on either side of the road and with level, sparsely vegetated plains stretching off to meet them. Far away to the left or to the right a curling wisp of smoke was often the only discernible sign of some small hut or farmhouse nestled not far from the mountains themselves.

Along the highway an occasional *ranchero* tried to attract attention to the small birds he offered for sale but which could not legally be carried across the border. Luis recalled with amusement stories about parrots, purchased from just such hawkers as these, whose heads had been dipped in liquor until they were so drunk they passed out. Then, hidden in the bottom of a purse or some other container, they had snoozed their way peacefully to American citizenship without any rude squawks to arouse the curiosity of a disapproving customs inspector.

Luis's van, however, carried nothing illegal. But this fact was shortly to prove quite irrelevant in circumstances where it ought to have been relevant. For while the travelers could not yet see it, only a few miles ahead of them all traffic was being stopped at a roadblock imposed by the Mexican Federal Police. It was there, all too soon, that the warm reminiscences of gracious Mexican hospitality would be jarringly dissolved into a nightmare of fear.

What a pity! The fact was that hospitality was as native to Mexico as a sombrero. When Luis thought of hospitality, it immediately evoked the frail image of Julia Olverda Anguiano and the simple clay-brick home in which she lived back in San Felipe. She was his wife's grandmother and must by now have been in her nineties. But one could not enter her home without the warmest of welcomes and an immediate offer of food or drink. Even the family dog which loudly greeted all visitors in the tiny vestibule just inside the front door seemed to reflect the friendly spirit of that household. But Julia could no longer really care for the needs of visitors herself. For that matter, she could no longer walk. And the sight of her shuffling her way on hands and knees across the central patio of her home, in order to be of some small service to her guests, furnished Luis with a touching recollection. Clearly, in the slender form and weather-beaten face of this venerable Mexican woman there pulsed the true spirit of the graceful Mexican saying, "Mi casa es su casa!" — "My house is your house!"

No less hospitable were "los primos" — the cousins. Sacrosantos Mongaras, called "Moreno" for his dark complexion, was the one with whom Luis had actually stayed. He owned a meat market and had facilities which the relatives deemed suitable for the comfort of their visitor from America. But wherever he had gone during those five rainy days, Luis was not only welcomed but fed.

Carnitas, sopa, quesadillas, chicharrón, chorizo, tostadas — these foods and more besides had been eagerly thrust upon him by people whose material means were far less than his own. That was the Mexican way, and not to eat was to offend. It was all part of a spirit which Luis deeply valued and which powerfully colored his conception of Mexico, the land of his own forebears.

But the country also had its more sinister side, and this facet of its character now stood athwart the highway in plain view.

"It's a roadblock!" The tone in Angel's voice was slightly edgy.

"It's the ___ *Policía Federal,*" snorted Octavio, salting the observation with a Spanish profanity.

Luis pulled the van to a stop behind a large tractor-trailer rig that blocked his lane. About a dozen armed federal policemen milled about the area or interrogated drivers. Luis reached for his papers in the tray in front of his dashboard.

"Don't do that," warned Octavio.

"I was only getting my papers out."

"Don't offer them anything unless they ask for it."

The rig in front of them was allowed to drive on, but their van was ordered to the side of the road. A lean federal policeman whose face strongly hinted at a streak of cold viciousness approached on the driver's side, a machine gun slung under his right arm.

"Get out."

Luis dismounted. As he did so, he felt an elbow in his stomach. *That must have been an accident,* he thought nervously.

"Back that way," the policeman ordered. On the way to the rear of the van there was another elbow in the ribcage.

That was NOT an accident. The tension in Luis mounted.

"Right there."

A pickup truck was parked behind the van. As Luis turned to face the rear of the van, his own back toward the other vehicle, for the third time an elbow met his body.

"What's wrong?" Luis asked.

"You're an American, aren't you?" The policeman's voice dripped with disdain.

"Yes." Luis now noticed the machine gun pointed directly toward him.

"We don't like you. You're a *pocho.*" The word signified someone whose abilities in the Spanish language were defective.

A fourth jab with the elbow was followed by a stream of abuse. The policeman crudely insulted Luis's mother and father, pungently suggesting illegitimacy as well as every other foul characteristic which a depraved person might be expected to possess.

As the supply of invective neared exhaustion, a second federal policeman approached the spot where the two of them were standing. He was taller and stouter than the first man, and he also brandished a machine gun. By this time Luis had noticed this weapon in the hands of all of the men who were manning the roadblock. Some of them even from a distance made a point of turning their lethal instrument in his direction.

As if on cue, the leaner policeman drifted off to be replaced by his bulkier comrade. A new torrent of insults poured out punctuated by obscenities. Luis held his tongue.

They want me to get hot so they can do something, he thought. The *Policía Federal* had a notorious reputation which they had richly earned. On isolated stretches of highway like this one, it would have meant nothing to them to riddle an innocent victim with bullets and to report that he had resisted arrest. Luis made up his mind not to grant them even the slightest excuse to do so.

His time apparently up, the large man gave way to a much shorter officer with plain, undistinguished features. Like all the others, he sported the omnipresent machine gun draped under one arm.

"What's your name?"

"Luis Rodriguez."

"Where are you from?"

"Dallas, Texas."

"Why are you in Mexico?"

"I was visiting my wife's grandmother."

"Her name?"

"Julia Olverda Anguiano."

"Where does she live?"

"San Felipe, Guanajuato."

"How long have you been down there?"

"Five days."

A few more stern questions terminated the interview. The absence of abuse made even this sharp interrogation seem like a kind of oasis, but the respite was soon over.

The next representative of the *Policía* was hardly more than a teenage kid, but trying hard to project a macho image in the American Army fatigue jacket by which his skinny frame was enveloped. As he paraded the full range of his obscene vocabulary in an obvious effort to exceed the vulgarity of his predecessors, Luis suppressed an urge to invite him to lay aside his machine gun and confront him on more equal terms. He would have dearly liked to extend a similar invitation to the others, too, but there was something about this scrawny, foul-mouthed boy that aroused the impulse more distinctly. He pushed the thought away.

Then, like some wind-up doll whose mechanism has run down, the youth walked off and, temporarily at least, Luis was left alone. Or so he thought.

The fear grew. *They're going to plant something on me so they can arrest me! Or they're going to beat me! Or kill me!*

The loathsome conditions of some obscure Mexican jail were an appalling thought. Luis knew only too well the difficulty and expense with which arrested Americans had been extricated from such places. But a severe beating could have consequences even more disastrous and long-lasting. And the machine guns! How easily they could eliminate the inconvenience of a complaint to consular authorities back in Dallas! For that reason these weapons were the most probable means for terminating this interview. Luis's skin crawled.

"They're a bunch of ____, aren't they?" The voice from behind him startled him.

There was a man sitting in the flatbed of the pickup truck to his rear. Luis had not even noticed him before. But for all Luis knew, he too might be a federal policeman since, with the exception of the youth in the fatigue jacket, the *Policía Federal* wore no uniforms.

It was unwise, therefore, to say too much. Luis gave the man the most imperceptible of nods. They *were* an odious lot, but he had better not say so too plainly.

Then he thought of his family. In his mind's eye he could see Feliz and his two boys, Viviano and Raul. He could feel the tug of the house that was home to him. But just now everything seemed unutterably far away.

I'll never see them again. The thought pushed its way unbidden into his consciousness. The unreasoning hostility he had just faced seemed like the savagery of a wild beast. It was as though his ears were ringing with the roar of a hungry lion which had now found its prey.

It *had* found its prey! For behind the animosity of a few well-armed federal policemen lay the profound hostility of a malevolent Power. More than once that implacable Foe had sought the irreparable ruin of the Latino man who, at this moment, felt very, very much alone.

2
Thunderbird

To the casual observer there was nothing in particular to distinguish Luis from the typical Hispanic male of the Southwestern United States. Even the *Policía Federal* could not have detected anything extraordinary about the individual upon whom they had trained their guns and their verbal abuse. The Chicano *viajero,* or tourist, from across the border was a common enough sight in Mexico, and the *Policía* saw them by the scores. It was true, of course, that a certain resentment smoldered just beneath the surface toward people whose racial roots were Mexican but who had attained the coveted privilege of American citizenship. But none of this set Luis significantly apart from countless others to whom he might have been superficially compared.

But there *was* a difference. In fact, it was a difference so profound and far-reaching that if it could have been explained to these hostile interrogators they would have regarded it as preposterously beyond belief. From their own perspective they reacted to him with an arrogance and antipathy that sprang solely from their personal inclinations. It would have startled them to learn that they served as mere pawns on a real-life chessboard where the issues at stake far transcended their own petty horizons. It would have startled them indeed, and it might have left them stunned with a kind of terrified incredulity.

The road on which they had intercepted Luis was not the only road upon which he had experienced the kind of high drama to which these men were so utterly blind. There had been another highway one time, years before, where the perceived realities of life met the unperceived realities in an incident that Luis was never able to forget. By any reasonable standard, however, he ought to have forgotten it the very next day. That he did not was a striking tribute to its extraordinary effect. For at the time, Luis had been drunk.

"Can I help you?" The filling-station attendant leaned over to speak through the window of the Buick Luis was driving.

"Yeah. Let me have some regular." He ordered several gallons, blinking his eyes from lack of sleep and too much beer.

It was well past midnight. Highway 83 out of McAllen, in far South Texas, was not likely to offer many other refueling stops at this hour of the night, so he had better get his gas now while he could. Besides, he wanted to wash up. Some cold water on the face might serve to rouse him a bit for the 40-mile trip to Harlingen that lay ahead.

With somewhat unsteady step, Luis followed the attendant into the station, which also doubled as a small store. He bought some cigarettes and went outside and around the corner to the tiny washroom. Upon emerging, only very slightly revived, he was returning to the car when he encountered the attendant again.

"You're in no condition to drive."

"I'll be all right."

"If you want to you could pull the car over there and get some sleep." The attendant indicated a portion of the lot on the east side of the building.

"No, no. I'm okay. I've got friends in Harlingen waiting for me."

"You shouldn't go on. You're drunk."

The service station man, like Luis, was a Latino. It occurred to Luis that if he did what was suggested, he might wake up without his cash. The attendant seemed unduly solicitous.

"I've gotta go. Don't worry about me. I have to make it back to Harlingen tonight."

Brushing aside renewed objections, Luis climbed back behind the wheel of the Buick and pulled out of the filling station's lot. Instinctively, despite his condition, he knew he ought not to be driving. But at 20 years of age such considerations usually made little if any headway against his plans. He was going back to Harlingen and that was all there was to it!

Only a short distance beyond the station he stopped for a traffic light. Across the intersection, coming from the opposite direction, a Thunderbird had also stopped for the light. Whether it was white in color Luis could never later be perfectly sure, but the impression that it was always remained.

The effect of the cold water was gone already. Luis's head drooped toward the steering wheel and he momentarily lost consciousness. At the same time his foot relaxed its pressure on the brake pedal and the Buick, which was an automatic, drifted slowly out into the intersection.

Suddenly the honking of a horn snapped him awake again. It was the Thunderbird, still stopped for the light. Luis found himself almost to the middle of the road that bisected the highway, a perfect target for any car coming from his right. Fortunately, at that hour of the night, none was coming.

The light changed. The Thunderbird started forward and, as they passed, Luis reached his hand through his open window to give the driver — whom he could not see — a grateful wave. From the other vehicle there was no response of any kind.

Then a peculiar thing happened. Just beyond the intersection the Thunderbird made a U-turn. As Luis watched through his rearview mirror, it retraced its path through the stoplight and began to follow him down the highway.

Oh, no! Luis groaned inwardly. *Just what I need! The police!* But there was a small incongruity. Did the police in South Texas drive Thunderbirds?

Luis's mind at the moment was a bit too groggy to grapple with an inconsistency like this. As the Thunderbird followed him along the road, the blackness behind that vehicle's windshield was all that Luis could make out. Not even the outline of a face or a form was visible to him. For all he knew, the car *might* have been driven by a policeman.

If it were, this would be a distinctly sour note on a trip which up till now had been a ball. Saturday had expired at midnight and, at the moment, Friday afternoon seemed like several days ago. That was when he, Porfirio, and Jorge had gotten off from their jobs in Dallas. It was easy to forget about the endless round of corn dogs and frozen dinners they were employed to prepare. They were excited by the prospect of a trip to "the valley," as the region around Harlingen and McAllen was commonly known. It would be a fun weekend.

After picking up Porfirio's wife and two young children, the five of them had headed south on highway 77 in the Buick, which was Jorge's. Harlingen, where Porfirio had relatives, was their destination. It was somewhere around 4 A.M. when they had pulled into the driveway of the modest house where his mother lived. Only a few hours later, after the stores opened, the trio had purchased their first six-pack of beer. Then they had begun cruising the city to see whatever sights Porfirio thought it worth their while to see.

Luis had been drinking ever since he was 15 years old. He was initiated into that manly art at a holiday party on a job where he worked as a delivery boy. But it did not make for a happy holiday when his mother, Julia Canales Rodriguez, saw her eldest son come home drunk for the first time. She was a large, robust woman and she had communicated her displeasure in forceful and explicit terms. But it was not to be the last time she saw him that way.

By now Luis was used to drinking three or four times a week. He had long ago learned to "kill a soldier every 15 minutes," as the barroom vulgarism put it. So naturally, when one of the trio suggested that they take a spin down to Reynosa, on the other side of the Mexican border, Luis was perfectly agreeable. After all, beer was cheaper in Reynosa than it was in Harlingen. With beer cans in hand, the friends had made the rounds of Reynosa's souvenir shops and had returned to Harlingen by way of McAllen.

Even that seemed quite some time ago. Later Luis had driven back to McAllen without Jorge or Porfirio. He was now retracing the route from there to Harlingen for the second time in a single day. For all practical purposes he had gone without sleep for most of two full days. Now his natural physical processes conspired with the effects of the alcohol to produce an increasingly powerful drowsiness. Staying awake at the wheel was simply an impossible task.

The Buick veered off onto the gravel which formed the shoulder of the blacktop, two-lane highway. The Thunderbird honked loudly, arousing Luis abruptly from his doze. Quickly he spun his steering wheel hard to the left and brought the car back onto the road.

A glance into his rearview mirror showed that the Thunderbird still trailed him, maintaining a distance of about six or seven car lengths between them. The situation struck Luis as distinctly odd.

But soon consciousness deserted him again and this time the car swerved into the opposite lane.

The horn of the Thunderbird blared vehemently.

Back in his own lane again, Luis felt grateful that there had been no oncoming traffic. Though there was little at this hour of the night, it was not unusual to find this road traveled very late by flatbed trucks loaded with oranges or grapefruits, or even by large rigs.

The process that had just occurred was repeated more times than Luis could later recall. Whenever he was overpowered by sleep and permitted the Buick to drift onto the shoulder or into the other lane, the Thunderbird would register its protest until Luis roused and brought his vehicle under control again.

It was apparent by this time that the driver behind him was no policeman. But who he was Luis could neither see nor imagine. The fact that the Thunderbird had originally been headed in the opposite direction only compounded the mystery. And in between dozes, Luis found his curiosity, if not his concern, mounting.

In one of the numerous small South Texas towns through which the highway passed, Luis made a decision. He would pull over to the side of the street and see if the Thunderbird would go around him.

It did not. For when Luis drove the Buick up to the curb of a deserted sidewalk, along which ran a row of darkened stores and buildings, the Thunderbird also pulled to a stop only a couple of car lengths behind.

There was no need for further investigation. Swiftly Luis accelerated the Buick back onto his route. As soon as he did so, the vehicle to his rear did likewise. Occasionally, between episodes of drowsiness, Luis would strain to catch sight in his mirror of some outline or form to this "companion" who was making Luis's journey his own. But always his gaze met the blank wall of darkness behind the other car's windshield, and nothing more.

Eventually the outskirts of Harlingen came into view. Over the entire span of some 40 miles, the Thunderbird had resolutely maintained its steady pace behind the wobbly course of the Buick. *What now?* Luis wondered. How far into the city would this unknown comrade carry his pursuit?

Inside Harlingen, at the intersection with highway 77, Luis turned north. So did the Thunderbird.

The Buick was now approaching the street where his friends were staying. Sighting the filling station which marked the turn, Luis took a right. So did the Thunderbird.

About three houses down, the Buick entered the driveway of the home which was its destination. Another three or four houses farther on, the street reached a dead end. The Thunderbird turned into the driveway behind Luis.

Stopping the car, Luis got out and started in the direction of the automobile to his rear. The least he could do was to offer his thanks for the assistance that had been so generously given to him. Yet as he walked toward the other vehicle, the darkness within it still hid even the trace of a figure or a face.

Abruptly the Thunderbird backed out of the driveway. Moving in the direction from which they had both come, it swiftly retraced its course to the highway where it turned, never to be seen by Luis again. Not even a brief honk on the by-now-familiar horn marked its departure.

What exactly he did next Luis did not afterward clearly recall. Whether he slept in the car or in the house he was not quite sure. The fog with which drunkenness clouds the memory took over and blotted out the remainder of that night. But the Thunderbird could not be forgotten. (Had it really been white?) Nor could Luis forget the strange determination of its unseen driver to see him safely to his journey's end.

But in the remembered events of that unusual night there lay an almost-eerie microcosm of the larger experience which, like anyone else, this young Latino would have called his "life." But he was in no condition to ponder that just now. Even after he sobered up the following day, what had transpired seemed only to be a remarkable, but isolated, incident.

But it was much more than that. With the passing years it would become increasingly apparent that behind the ordinary as well as the extraordinary events of Luis's experience, a struggle was taking place between forces about which he as yet understood only a very little.

Meanwhile, the question which persisted about the strange journey he had taken from McAllen to Harlingen was an obvious one. Who was the benevolent human being who had driven that Thunderbird? But perhaps the question should have been: Was it a human being at all?

3
Aura of Fear

From a superficial point of view, it was surprising that Luis did not conclude that the Thunderbird was driven by some otherworldly being. The previous generation of Hispanic Americans believed strongly in supernatural realities and in the impact they could have on the lives of ordinary people. But Luis was part of an emerging Latino culture which was both self-consciously proud of its roots and privately disdainful of the old-fashioned superstitions. Though younger Hispanics still retained much of their traditional reverence for the dignity of age, the American experience inclined them to smile condescendingly about matters which their ancestors would have treated with awe.

Yet as children they had felt the power of these older beliefs. Luis was no exception. Take the "witch" on Floyd Street. *La vieja mala*, as she was called in Spanish, had been an object of fear to him and to his two sisters, Mary and Christine. They often wished she did not live on the same street with them. No doubt the woman had been nothing more than a destitute old lady, living alone with her dogs. She made her meager living by collecting cardboard in a cart she pushed around and by selling the cardboard at a neighborhood paper house. But even this could seem sinister.

"If you're not good, " Luis's mother would warn her children, "*la vieja mala* will put you in her wagon and take you to her house."

Luis and his sisters suspected that the woman must have two or three bad kids tied up in her decrepit dwelling. They wanted no part of that! But in time, Luis and his childhood friends worked up enough courage to toss rocks at the unfortunate lady and to pull pranks on her. It was a kind of symbolic rebellion against the superstitious fear she aroused and against the beliefs of their elders. The lore of their Hispanic heritage was gradually being left behind.

Still, it wasn't as though the older generation had not tried to communicate their beliefs. They certainly had. And Luis would never forget the nights when stories were told on the front porch of his Floyd Street home. A kerosene lamp provided a kind of spooky illumination for the crowd of friends and neighbors who might gather there. With childlike wonder, Luis and his sisters would listen eagerly to the strange tales their mother or father could tell so well.

Who could forget the one about the man down in Mexico who loved to attend dances even though such activities were frowned on as frivolous and worldly? Julia, his mother, had recounted it more than once.

"There was this man who loved to dance," she might begin. "He didn't care at all what other people said or thought. He liked to have his fun, so he never missed a dance.

"One day out in the fields, he heard two men talking about a dance which was to be held that night. He couldn't quite see their faces, but he listened to what they said and he made up his mind to go.

"That night he started off down the road in the direction he had heard them say. Pretty soon he saw one of these two men on the road ahead of him, so he walked faster and caught up with him. It was dark and he still couldn't see his face, but he walked along beside him anyway.

" 'How far is it to the dance?' he asked.

" 'Not far,' the man answered.

"They walked on some more and he asked again, 'How far is it?'

" 'Not far,' the man said.

"After a while he heard the sound of music, so he was sure that the dance was not very far away. But they kept walking and walking, and always he heard the music and thought they were almost there.

"Finally he turned to the man again to ask how much farther it was, and he got the same answer: 'Not far.'

"All at once he looked down at the man's feet. But the man didn't have any feet — he had hooves instead!

" 'Oh, my God!' he cried. 'Where is this devil taking me?'

"Just then the man he had been walking with disappeared. He could not see him anymore, but there was a smell in the air like acid. Now he was by himself. Suddenly he looked around and saw that he was deep in the woods. There was no road there or anything else. He was terribly scared and his heart pounded inside him as he tried to find his way home again. He didn't care if he ever went to another dance in his whole life!"

Luis couldn't blame the man for that! He only hoped he got home all right. The kerosene lamp would flicker a bit and the children would ask for more.

Perhaps it would be their father, also named Luis, who told the next one. And this time they might hear about the young man who flirted with anything which wore a skirt. He whistled indiscriminately at young women and old, at married ladies and unmarried ladies. And then one day he saw an absolutely enchanting female figure walking ahead of him across a bridge. Her shape was gorgeous, her dress exquisite, and long tresses of beautiful hair extended well down her back.

Quickening his pace, he whistled and called after her.

"Chiquita! Bonita! Mamasita!" he cried. "¿Adónde vas? Espérame!" ("Where are you going? Wait for me!")

At last he caught up with her on the bridge. But when he did so, the figure turned its head toward him and he found himself staring horrified at a hideous skull!

Stories like these formed part of a common tradition which one could expect to hear repeated in much the same way in many Hispanic households. But Luis and Julia Rodriguez also drew frequently and graphically upon that special fund of lore which pertained directly to their immediate family.

Julia, for example, would say, "Your great granddaddy on your father's side used to play the fiddle and dance for a living. He often did this every night from Thursday through Sunday. On one of those nights he was getting dressed when his wife came up to him.

" 'Where are you going to play tonight?' she asked.

" 'I don't know and I don't care,' your granddaddy said. 'I need money real bad right now, so I'd play for the devil himself if he'd pay me!'

"After he said that he went out into the dark. It was awfully late when he finally came back to the house. His face was pale and he looked dreadful.

" 'What happened?' his wife asked him. She was frightened by his appearance.

" 'I played for the devil tonight,' he told her, 'and I saw José and Pepe and Maria and the people I used to know when they were alive. It was terrible. I think I was in hell.'

"That night your granddaddy died, and they say that when he passed away his eyes were bulging out of his head!"

Now *there* was a story that struck home! Luis could not help being impressed that his own great grandfather had learned the folly of serving the devil. It was easy for him, as a child, to decide never to do a thing like that. But real life was considerably more complex than this simple tale suggested. Luis was destined to learn that there was more than one way to "play" for the devil.

To the discerning observer it would have been clear that Hispanic culture sought to enforce morality through the agency of fear. Those who carelessly disregarded accepted values might find themselves caught in the coils of satanic power or confronting grisly experiences whose horror they would never forget. That there could be some higher form of motivation for right conduct was a thought which such stories did not convey. But because the older generation had correctly sensed that the universe was moral, they believed strongly in the fear-ridden tales of retribution which they relayed to their offspring.

One of the most striking figures in the family's narrations was Luis's grandfather — his mother's father — Viviano Canales. As a young boy his name was associated with a bizarre experience which had happened to a *compadre* of his father. This *compadre* (a "godfather" for one of the elder Canales' children) was a man of deep poverty whom others had often assisted in times of need.

One night he had been walking down a lonely road in the Mexican countryside when he saw ahead of him a bull whose two eyes were glowing like coals. At first the bull appeared to be charging him, but before it reached the *compadre* it disappeared into the ground. In the days that followed, this peculiar episode reoccurred on the same road two or three times more, with the bull always disappearing into the ground at what seemed to be precisely the same spot. At the last occurrence, the thought dawned on the *compadre* that this was a sign intended for him. Perhaps the point at which the creature vanished into the earth concealed something of value.

Spurred on by this hunch, the man rushed to a nearby farmhouse to borrow a shovel. But he did not share his expectations with the farmer who loaned him this tool. Instead he dashed off to dig by himself. Presently, just as he had hoped, he unearthed a considerable treasure. But the treasure was too big for him to carry away in his arms. Now he needed a wheelbarrow.

Hastily he retraced his steps to the farmhouse. His heart was thrilled with the joy of his discovery and excited thoughts cascaded through his mind.

Now I can buy my children shoes, he told himself, and there will always be food on my table! I can have my friends in for dinner and I can repay them for the things they have done for me!

When he arrived at the farmhouse, he reported what he had found and asked the farmer for his wheelbarrow.

"Do you need any help?" the farmer inquired.

A sudden burst of greed surged over the *compadre's* soul.

"No, no!" he insisted. "I can handle it by myself! Just let me use your wheelbarrow!"

"I'm so sorry," replied the farmer, "but I loaned it to Señor Canales. You'll have to get it from him."

The *compadre* hastened off to the farm owned by Viviano Canales' father, which was a little distance away. There at last he obtained the needed wheelbarrow. But by the time he returned to the site of his digging, the treasure was gone. Shaken and sad, he resumed once more his poverty-stricken life. He realized bitterly that he had lost everything because he had allowed his good fortune to be tarnished by greed.

As a young lad, Viviano Canales might have learned a lesson from a tale like this. But as a grown man he displayed a distinct trace of the skeptical spirit which would mark his grandson Luis, whose middle name in fact would be Canales. One story in particular revealed this quality of mind, and for once the incident was probably true.

While Luis's mother was still a young girl, Viviano and his household were following the crops in an agricultural region of Texas. That state was now Viviano's adopted home. As he was about to move on to labor in the fields of a nearby town, a friend gave him a warning. While he was working there, he must be sure to purchase his food supplies on Saturday afternoon well before sundown. There was — so his friend informed him — a "devil" that lurked in the woods just outside that town and who relieved the farmhands of their purchases if they passed that way after dark.

"He won't get anything from me!" Viviano had stoutly declared. "I don't intend to feed any devil the food I worked hard to buy for my own family!"

He soon had the opportunity to prove his determination. One Saturday evening he and his family were leaving the town. In their wagon they were making their way through the deepening darkness back to the lodgings where the field hands stayed. As he gently prodded his animal forward, Viviano happened to notice on the road well ahead a figure who seemed to be waiting for them. In the gloom of the trees which overshadowed their route, he could make out little about this sinister person. Yet a tiny red glow revealed unmistakably that he was puffing steadily on a cigarette!

When the wagon reached the spot, the figure — which had withdrawn behind a tree — suddenly leaped out into the road. He was an awesome sight indeed, dressed from head to foot in a devil's suit which glittered under the light of the moon and was complete even to the horns on his head and the fluttering cape on his back. It was not hard to imagine the terror he must have inspired in the numerous farm hands who had encountered him previously on this path.

But Viviano Canales was undismayed. He had already concluded that a creature from hell would not while away its idle moments with an earthly cigarette! So he quickly dismounted from his wagon to confront this "devil," and in vivid language he offered to give him a beating he was not likely to forget. This was more than the "devil" had bargained for. Instead of challenging his intended victim, he beat a hasty (and some said permanent) retreat into the woods!

It would have been nice if all the devils of Hispanic tradition could have been so easily routed. It would have been even nicer if the real one could have been! But by a kind of irony it was the traditions themselves which served to conceal the true character of the being whose evil undertakings were incomparably more sophisticated than anything such tales disclosed.

There was nothing that Luis had heard during his childhood which really prepared him for the immense struggle with this being which lay ahead of him in the years to come. If anything, the stories he had been told actually weakened his power to resist.

So also did some of his earliest experiences. For as a young child Luis could not remain immune to the dread of the supernatural which was so much a part of his mental environment. And this aura of fear produced at least one eerie childhood recollection.

Behind the house on Floyd Street an alley ran east and west and furnished a convenient route to Swiss Avenue, where there was a drugstore. A little way down Swiss, around the corner on Skiles Street, there was also a general store called Cash Brothers, where everyone in the neighborhood traded. When Luis was sent to either of these stores it was natural for him to use the alleyway, but after dark he did so with a certain amount of apprehension.

A story which circulated among the residents of Floyd Street claimed that sometimes at night you could see a woman with a washboard sitting on a fence along the alleyway scrubbing clothes into a number 5 washtub! The possibility of encountering this apparition on one of his errands was a thought that haunted Luis's mind as he walked through the shadows. So vivid was this expectation that in later years he came to feel he had once actually seen this figure engaged in her nocturnal chores.

One evening there was a commotion in the alley. Luis ran out of his house to investigate. The police were there and an ambulance was parked near a side entrance to the drugstore. From the excited spectators Luis learned that a man had been shot during a robbery.

This was the last straw. Somehow this real-life experience added the final intolerable element of fear to that alleyway. From then on he avoided it completely at night and instead took a longer route across a nearby park. In doing this he was bearing testimony to the way in which the unreal can increase the fearfulness of the real.

Yet as early as the age of four or five Luis experienced his very first skeptical feelings. A storm was in the process of brewing and a huge black cloud hung threateningly over the Dallas skyline. When his parents saw this they were considerably agitated. His mother grabbed a butcher knife, placed it in Luis's hand, and brought him outside so he could "cut the storm in half."

"Mom, you can't cut that thing in half," Luis protested.

"Boy," his mother replied, "you don't understand the things of the world, because little kids can do great things!"

"Mom, let's go in the house 'cause the storm is going to hit us!"

"Cut it in a cross!" Julia insisted.

So as best he could Luis made two slash marks in the air in the general form of a crucifix and promptly scurried inside with the rest of the family. The storm came anyway, completely undeterred by the young boy's efforts to hex it, and that fact was duly registered on his impressionable personality. Not everything that his parents believed was borne out by the facts.

That was why Luis entertained serious doubts about an incident a few years later which was thought to involve the supernatural. His mother and father had been arguing inter-mittently for several days, and during an interlude Julia went into the bathroom and locked the door. After a few moments Luis and the rest of the family heard her utter a bloodcurdling scream.

Luis's father rushed immediately to the locked bathroom and got into it. When he came out, he ordered his children to run outside to head off any intruder they might see. Obediently Luis ran out one door and Mary and Christine ran out another, but the yard was as empty of strangers as the house was. What they would have done if it had not been, they never had the least idea!

Luis later recalled seeing his mother with both hands over her face. When she took them down her countenance dis-played three or four long, jagged scratches starting on her forehead and extending well down her cheeks. The wounds were exactly such as might have been made by sharp, pointed fingernails. According to Julia, a shadowy female figure had come out of the bathroom wall and had attacked her with a black hand, leaving behind the bloody marks on her face.

It was a frightening episode that troubled Luis long after its terror wore off. What had really happened? His mother did not wear her own fingernails long, yet no one else had seen a shape or a form of any kind. Had she done this to herself? That was not an easy conclusion for a child to reach, and Luis never quite reached it. But uncertainty inescapably remained.

As the years passed, Luis felt the tensions that arise when a person gradually outgrows a culture to which he nevertheless owes much. No doubt a great deal of what had been transmit-ted to him was simply not true. Yet at the same time Hispanic thought was much closer to reality than the outright naturalism and secularism which permeated Anglo-American society. With that innate common sense which often marks less sophisticated cultures, the Latino tradition insisted that life was more than the sum of its visible parts. It maintained that the natural world was intersected by a supernatural world from which men also drew real and genuine experiences. Luis was eventually to learn that here at least his heritage had not misled him.

Yet it remained true that for Hispanic people unseen realities were chiefly a source of fear and dread. There was little in their multiplied legends and anecdotes which pointed to any Source of benevolence which was unconditionally generous and good. According to the received wisdom, if a person prospered or succeeded, it was precisely because this was what he deserved.

From that perspective, the Thunderbird actually constituted an enigma. Perhaps it was not incredible that an extraterrestrial being had driven it. But Hispanic thought had no precedent for the wholly unmerited kindness which it had brought. In Latino tales such favors were never bestowed on drunks!

4
Half-Dollar for Nothing

Luis's experience with the Thunderbird did convey the impression that some benign Power was interested in his well-being. But Luis's initial encounter with this Power had occurred during his childhood. That encounter was so simple it had hardly seemed mysterious at all. Yet its simplicity was deceptive and served as a kind of mask which concealed a miracle of immense proportions. By comparison with this miracle, neither the Thunderbird incident nor any other event of Luis's life deserved to be mentioned in the same breath.

But the miracle almost never happened. This was because Luis's very existence had once hung by an exceedingly slender thread.

Luis was the oldest son in a family that eventually consisted of ten children, evenly divided between five boys and five girls. Only Mary and Christine were older than he, but the oldest child should have been a boy.

Julia had been pregnant with the infant who was to be her firstborn. As was common in Hispanic households, delivery was handled by a midwife. What motives prompted Luis's father to follow this practice were never known, but the use of a midwife nearly ended the Rodriguez family before it began.

The baby — a little boy — died at delivery. The mother almost died. But grandfather Viviano Canales recognized his daughter's serious condition and summoned an intern from nearby Baylor Hospital. The intern insisted that Julia be hospitalized immediately. Even then her life was only barely preserved.

Later the family traditions insisted that Viviano had been so furious with the midwife that he had wanted to take fatal vengeance on her. The dead infant would have been his first grandson, and the disappointment wounded him deeply. Death had proved a more formidable foe than the make-believe "devil" he had put to flight many years before.

But beyond the tears of grief, there was irony in the fact that if the child had lived he would almost certainly have been named Luis Canales. And if Julia had died, Luis himself would not have been born. Thus Luis Canales Rodriguez owed his very existence and identity to a tragedy that happened and to one that did not.

There was something about all this which seemed profound-ly significant to Luis in later years. It was as though some sovereign Hand had mysteriously anointed him with the gift of physical life and had appointed him, and not another, to bear the name he bore.

Luis's own birth took place in September of 1941, only a little more than two months before Pearl Harbor. Though his grandfathers on both sides had come from Mexico, the Rodriguez family was now an American family whose for-tunes were permanently cast with the land their forebears had chosen. In 1943, not long after the birth of another son, Robert Arthur, the elder Luis was drafted into the United States Navy. While he was gone, Julia bore him his third son, Juan Carlos.

Three years elapsed during which Julia ran the household alone. Despite the fact that there were now five children, one a babe in arms, she did this with the competence and self-assurance which so strongly marked her nature.

Luis often recalled a striking example of his mother's capacity to care for her offspring. Julia was seated on a crowded bus, holding John in her lap, and with Robert riding beside her. Luis, Mary, and Christine occupied the seat just behind her. Two well-dressed Anglo women got on, but the vehicle was full and they had no place to sit. The bus driver came back to the seat where the three children were sitting.

"Give these white ladies your seat," he ordered, and promptly began to shove them toward the aisle.

Julia rose from her seat and her eyes flashed.

"You leave my children alone!" she warned him. "That's their seat and they have as much right to sit there as those white ladies!"

The conductor surveyed her for a moment. She was a large woman and he was dubious of the consequences that might follow from enforcing his demand. Without a word he returned to the front of the bus. The Anglo women stood. But when Mrs. Rodriguez rang for her stop, the driver deliberately went a half-block beyond it before letting the family off. This act entitled him to a further remonstrance from the indignant mother.

"My husband is in the service," she informed him as she got off, "and he's fighting for his country so you can be free. You're the kind of man they ought to send overseas and let my husband come home!" With that, she exited the vehicle with her children. The incident became a favorite family anecdote.

But this spirit of proud independence soon manifested itself in Julia's son. Her four younger sisters, Maria, Luisa, Carolina, and Senona, doted on him and called him a "beautiful doll." That probably didn't help matters. And when Grandmother Canales passed away, Granddad Viviano tried to fill the void by turning his affections toward his grandson. One benefit to Luis from this new grandfatherly regard was his first pair of cowboy boots! One disadvantage was the reinforcement of a deep streak of stubbornness.

An early demonstration of this trait occurred in catechism class. During one of the first sessions Luis managed to displease the Catholic Sister who presided over the instruction. She proceeded to discipline him by twisting and pulling his ear. It was a tactical blunder. Luis promptly got up and went home. He reported the incident to his mother and announced his intention not to go back.

Within a day or two, the neighborhood *Padre* descended on the Rodriguez domicile for one of his rare calls. Somewhat imperiously he informed Julia that her son was to be back in catechism class the very next day. It was another tactical blunder. Mrs. Rodriguez succinctly retorted that he ought not to look for her son tomorrow as she was quite sure he would not be there!

He wasn't, either. But later, when his friend Jesse became an altar boy, Luis was debarred from this role because he had missed his first communion. The twinge of regret he felt was never completely forgotten.

By the time Luis was old enough to attend public school, his rebel instincts were sharply honed. Despite his youth, he soon verified the truth that the career of a sinner begins in his childhood.

The building that was once Stephen F. Austin Elementary School still stands in Dallas at the corner of Washington Street and Gaston Avenue. Among the countless children who have entered its portals, few have been more adverse to the educational process than was Luis. He failed his first semester due to an intense dislike for the disciplines of a classroom. He much preferred the "jungle."

The "jungle" was a weedy area situated on the banks of a creek that once ran a few blocks along Hall Street, not far from the Rodriguez's Floyd Street home. Telephone poles had been laid there in piles, and it became a favorite spot for the neighborhood children to play. Whenever the impulse struck him, which was quite often, Luis would escape to the "jungle" and forfeit a day's education. There was a kind of symbolism in that, for it was not only as a child that Luis would prefer a "jungle" to the benefits of urgently needed instruction.

At first Luis would stay at the "jungle" just long enough so that he could no longer be sent to school. Then he would go home. Later he devised a quicker way of avoiding the class-room: he would jump into the creek and go home soaking wet! This condition effectively guaranteed another day off.

Exasperated, Julia began sending Luis to school with Mary and Christine. But hardly did they get him through the front door than Luis would sneak out the back. When his sisters started conducting him directly to his classroom, Luis would use recess or the lunch break as the occasion for his escape.

In time, however, the young boy settled into a reasonably regular attendance at school. But this concession to form did not signal a newfound thirst for knowledge. Instead, the classroom became a fresh arena for mischievous conduct and for new displays of headstrong self-will.

Miss Nichols, one of Luis's first teachers, had the misfortune of discovering these traits at firsthand. It was ironic that one of their first clashes was over the word "would."

"Read that word, Luis," Miss Nichols directed.

"I can't," Luis replied.

"Yes, you can. Read it!"

"I can't."

"Read it!"

"I can't, Miss Nichols."

"Luis, you'll either read that word now, or you'll stay after school and write it on the blackboard."

But Luis would not read "would." A session at the blackboard that afternoon made the word a permanent part of his vocabulary.

It did not, however, improve his artwork.

During one classroom drawing session, when water paints were being used, Luis drew a stick figure to represent a person.

"Luis," Miss Nichols instructed, "don't draw a stick figure. Draw it so that it actually looks like a real person."

"That's the best I can do, Miss Nichols."

"No, it isn't. Draw it right."

When Miss Nichols was summoned from the room, Luis improved the occasion by splashing his water paints extensively over the classroom walls. Upon the teacher's return, Luis's classmates promptly pointed to him as the culprit. Then followed a swift trip to the principal's office, where a memorable whipping was duly administered.

That was only the first installment. Julia was called to the scene to survey her son's handiwork. She repeated the principal's procedure on Luis at home.

Miss Nichols despaired of her recalcitrant pupil's future. "Luis will never learn," she once told Miss Williams, whose classroom Luis later graced at another school. But Miss Williams was not so sure. Though she was a strict disciplinarian herself, she entertained a more hopeful view of Luis's prospects. In fact, the day came when she told Luis what his former teacher had said. In contrast Miss Williams stressed her own positive expectations. But by that time Luis had already met another Teacher whose aspirations for him were even higher than Miss Williams's.

Though it was not evident at the time, this childhood waywardness was preparing the ground for a supernatural event which would change Luis's life permanently. The word "sin" was not yet a working part of his vocabulary, but the boy knew in his heart that he was far from a perfect child. He also knew that disobedience to authority could provoke severe retribution. Gradually he was drifting toward a remarkable rendezvous with the highest Authority of all.

Beneath Luis's stubborn exterior there was also a capacity for tenderness. A ceremony was held one day in the auditorium at Stephen F. Austin School in honor of a retiring principal. Auld Lang Syne was sung and some of the teachers cried. Luis could sense that it was somehow a sorrowful occasion for them, and in his own childlike way he felt that sorrow too. More than once, in later years, he recalled this gathering when he happened to pass by the school, and the sadness would touch him briefly all over again.

But such somber experiences were rare in Luis's carefree early days. When the family moved to Chestnut Street, Luis transferred to Alamo School. There he happily recognized true kindred spirits in three new boyhood buddies — Jesse, Manuel, and Matthew. Together the foursome managed to pool their not inconsiderable talents for mischief. A quartet they were, but jarringly out of harmony with their teachers' desire for proper behavior.

In music class the four often joined together to sing a song distinctly different from the one their music instructor was playing.

"Someone's not singing right," the teacher would complain.

A half dozen fingers would point at Jesse, Manuel, Matthew, and Luis.

Luis's father had by now returned from the Navy. He reported, with a twinkle in his eye, that the closest he had come to actual combat was the time his ship had almost fired on a sister ship whose communications had failed. The bus driver might have smiled sardonically if he had heard that one! But the senior Luis enjoyed the respect of his own children.

Like Julia, he insisted on the dignity of the family. There was, for example, the time that Luis had gone to an aunt's house for dinner.

"Don't do that again," his father had warned him. "I don't want people to say I can't feed my own kids."

Even after Luis got older, his dad would send him off to the barbershop with words like, "Go get yourself a haircut, boy. People are going to say there goes Luis's son and he can't even afford to get him a haircut."

Or he might say, "Tell your mother to go buy you a pair of shoes, boy. Those have holes in them and people are going to say we can't buy you a pair of shoes."

Most of the shoes came from Goodwill anyway. Working primarily on construction jobs, Luis Sr. could not always count on employment, and supporting his growing family was no easy task. Unknown to his father, Luis occasionally helped the family budget in an unauthorized fashion. A few times he went to the Goodwill store to try on a pair of shoes and simply walked out leaving his old ones on the rack.

Detection by his dad would probably have brought swift punishment. Though he rarely whipped his children, he could discipline them in ways hard to forget. For failing to do an assigned chore, for example, he would tell Luis to get two bricks and kneel on them with his face in the corner. After periods ranging up to two hours in this position, almost any chore seemed like a pure delight!

One time the paternal correction took a particularly ingenious form. Manor Bakery used to deliver to homes and allow their customers to buy on credit. Luis's mother would often buy cinnamon rolls, which Luis regarded as exquisitely delicious.

He was regularly inclined to ask for more than he was allowed and once made a terrific scene when his request was denied. As punishment, his father insisted that he eat two whole packages. They made Luis sick, and after that he no longer had the slightest interest in cinnamon rolls!

It was an effective technique, not altogether unlike one that would be used by that Authority under whose discipline Luis would soon find himself. But his mother always afterward blamed her son's upset stomachs on the cinnamon rolls and used to give him grapefruit juice and salt to drink.

Luis never felt he wanted parents other than the ones he had. It never occurred to him in these years that he really needed the kind of paternal direction which no merely human parent could ever provide. His father and mother loved him, of this he felt sure, and the discipline they exercised was one proof of this.

Neither parent took any special interest in Luis's recreational activities, nor did he expect them to. His father had no interest in sports or in the out-of-doors, and Luis was later to pick up these interests entirely on his own. At a somewhat older age, when he participated in a marbles tournament, he felt no sense of disappointment when neither of his parents came to watch. The concept of a Parent who was deeply concerned with the smallest matters in His children's lives was still quite foreign to the young boy.

Luis Sr. and Julia Rodriguez attended the Catholic Church only rarely. But Mary and Christine went regularly, and so for a time did Luis. Often he accompanied his altar boy companion, Jesse, and Jesse's mother, Chencha. Despite the hindrance of not being properly catechized, he enjoyed church and quickly learned when to stand or kneel during the Mass and how to make the responses which the rest of the congregation made. But because he did not go to confession, he was not allowed to go forward and kneel at the railing to receive the wafer which the priest administered to the worshipers. This gave him the unhappy feeling of being left out.

Sometimes Luis accompanied Jesse to confession and waited outside while his friend went into the confessional. The whole procedure seemed strange to Luis and somehow irrelevant. When he would ask, Jesse would try to explain what it was all about, but his answers never really impressed Luis. Instinctively, even at that young age, he sensed that confessions made to another human being were pointless.

As time passed, however, for reasons he could never later recall, Luis stopped attending the Catholic Church. There was no pressure at home for him to resume his attendance, and the way was prepared for a decisive turn in the course of his life.

One Sunday, in the early evening, a pickup truck was going slowly through the neighborhood and happened to pass Luis's house while Luis was outside. In the bed of the pickup sat a schoolboy acquaintance named Wally Mitchell.

"Hey, Luis!" Wally yelled. "Want to go to church?"

"Maybe," Luis called back. "Let me ask my mother."

"If you want to do it, go ahead," was Julia's reply. Luis hopped into the truck with Wally.

A less impressive site for a "church" would have been hard to imagine. Situated on Jeffries Street between Aikens and Dawson, the building which the children entered was a clapboard structure topped by a peaked tin roof. The few windows contained no glass. In warm weather they were completely open to the outside air. When it was cold, boards of masonite were inserted to seal in the heat from a single wood-burning stove. Stark wooden benches, individually handmade, were arranged on either side of a center aisle. A sturdily constructed lectern occupied the center of the space in front of the benches, flanked on the right by a piano and on the left by some cabinets designed to hold books.

This makeshift meeting place occupied a fairly substantial piece of land. On the south side of this lot, toward Dawson Street, stood a large two-story house which had probably once been a moderately fashionable residence. On the north side, toward Aikens Street, stood a simple three-room dwelling which qualified as one of the "shotgun" houses which dotted the deteriorating neighborhood. Just past this structure was an open space and a large tree.

Strangely enough, the "church" had begun under that tree. There, years before, two women named Mrs. Lewelling and Mrs. Humphreys had often assembled a congregation of children. This audience was enthralled by the charming Bible stories the two ladies told. When at last the simple clapboard building had been erected, its very existence must have seemed to the women to suggest a kind of hopeful permanence. But they could hardly have guessed what lay ahead.

None of this history really mattered to Luis. Mrs. Lewelling and Mrs. Humphreys were gone, but he liked Horace and Dorothy Gill who presided over things in their place. And he liked young Ray Jones, who drove the pickup truck and preached. In contrast to the incomprehensible Latin which was used in the Mass at the Catholic Church, he enjoyed listening to things he could understand, and soon he was coming on a regular basis. The boys' club on alternate Friday nights, featuring films, refreshments, and games, was another attraction to which Luis happily responded. Naturally he had not the slightest notion that he had entered a magnetic field which pulsed with supernatural energy.

Then came the night of the half-dollar! The preacher at the Jeffries Street meeting was expounding on a theme that could have been easily summed up in the Biblical declaration that "the gift of God is eternal life in Christ Jesus our Lord."

In order to make his subject as vivid and real as possible for his young audience, the speaker held up a 50-cent piece. He announced that he would give it away freely just as God gave eternal life freely. Luis's eyes widened when he realized that someone was about to receive what seemed to Luis like a substantial amount of money. But when the opportunity to take it came, another boy went up and got the 50 cents.

Luis regretted that he had missed such a financially promising opportunity! He was determined that the next time a half-dollar was available just for the taking, he would be out of his seat quicker than anyone. But the next time never came. Luis never got a half-dollar for nothing at the clapboard church.

What he got was infinitely greater.

The lesson behind the half-dollar had deeply affected Luis's thinking. It was perfectly clear to the young boy that he needed eternal life. He had heard about hell from his earliest years, but the preachers at the church made it a real issue. Luis certainly did not want to go to hell when he died (which he assumed he would not for a long time), but he felt he ought to get ready just in case. It was obviously much better to go to heaven. But to do that he had to possess eternal life. And, like the half-dollar, it was free.

That was why, after one of the Jeffries Street meetings, Luis lingered around the front benches while the other children rushed out to play. The speaker had suggested that anyone who was interested in getting God's gift could stay behind and talk about it, and Luis wanted to talk.

The preacher sat down with him on one of the benches. In simple terms he explained that the Lord Jesus Christ had died for Luis's sins and was only asking Luis to trust Him by accepting the gift which His death had provided. Behind the words Luis was hearing echoed the clear statements of Jesus Himself: "Verily, verily, I say to you, he who believes on Me has everlasting life," and, "Whoever wants to, let him take the water of life freely."

Then it happened. The most decisive supernatural event of Luis's entire life transpired while he sat on that rude, hand-made bench. With complete childlike simplicity Luis opened his heart to eternal life. In that instant, the Creator of the universe became his own heavenly Father. The ramifications of this profound experience would be incalculable. Luis could not have guessed them even if he had tried.

But he didn't try. He simply ran outside and played.

5
Target for Attack

The "shotgun" house situated next to the clapboard church was the home of an elderly lady and a pack of dogs. Unlike the "witch" on Floyd Street, no one thought of her as *una vieja mala*. But her dogs could be dangerous when aroused.

One day Luis and several other boys were killing time outside the clapboard church before one of the Friday night meetings. Through the makeshift wooden fence which surrounded the woman's yard they were poking sticks at the dogs, and they embellished this pastime by throwing rocks at them and making faces.

Suddenly one of the animals leaped the fence. It headed straight for Luis's schoolboy chum, Manuel, who managed to jump over the dog with impressive youthful agility.

Luis was not so fortunate. Before the dog could be driven off it had inflicted four wounds on his left leg, two on the top part of his thigh and two on the back of it. A scratch just above the left knee was a memento of its paw.

This happened not long after Luis's encounter with the generosity of his Maker. An observer with foresight might have seen the incident as symbolic of what lay ahead. The new life which had just recently begun for the young boy had aroused the hostility of an Adversary. And this Enemy's attack would be so ferocious that deep wounds would be left whose scars would never disappear. Yet, as with the attack by the dog, Luis himself would bear a responsiblity for what took place.

The assault began with a subtlety and sophistication that made it virtually unrecognizable at first. Luis continued for the next year or so to attend meetings at the clapboard church with spontaneous regularity. The preaching he heard there reinforced his assurance that he possessed eternal life. In his own childlike way he was aware that God cared for him. The genuineness he detected in people like the Gills and Ray Jones encouraged him to invite his brothers and sisters and friends to attend with him. But Luis's Enemy was already at work.

The companions which Luis had found at school provided his Foe with an opening wedge. The old quartet of Jesse, Manuel, Matthew, and Luis not only continued their mischief but found ways to escalate it. Once they managed to ring the school bell in the manner employed for a fire drill. They then dashed into the music room, where at the moment there was no teacher.

The spurious drill was aborted only because a buzzer located in the principal's office also had to ring. Of course, the principal did not ring it. Instead, she made the rounds of the classrooms, demanding to know who had sounded the alarm. Behind bland countenances, the four boys concealed their glee that they had completely escaped detection.

On the school grounds, the companions were bullies who coerced or manipulated people as they wished. They were especially proud of a scam which they had honed into a fine art. Matthew and Luis would challenge a third party to flip coins with them, and the one whose piece of money came down differently would win the other coins. But since Matthew and Luis could always manage to get opposite results from the toss, the third party invariably lost. The two partners collected a considerable amount of change from their gullible schoolmates before their "racket" was generally recognized.

Undiscouraged, they introduced a new competition in which they offered a one-on-one encounter. Like sheep asking to be sheared, their clientele returned and were regularly fleeced of their money, since either Matthew or Luis could easily control the way their coins came up. Without really thinking about it and without feeling any guilt, Luis had learned to cheat other people and was becoming conditioned to it. It was exactly what his Enemy desired.

Luis was seven or eight years old when he smoked his first cigarette. Another friend, named Jesse, became his partner in this youthful vice by sharing his packs with Luis. Four or five times they went to the "jungle" at Hall and Floyd Streets and smoked until they got sick.

Once he and Jesse were ambling down Oak Street when they encountered Jesse's dad at an intersection waiting for a bus. Swiftly Jesse deposited his lighted cigarette in his hip pocket to avoid detection and started talking to his father.

While the bus delayed its arrival, Jesse wiggled with growing discomfort. When the vehicle finally appeared and his father got on, the two boys dashed off around the corner with Jesse wildly beating his behind! Luis was extremely amused.

One nagging childhood concern for Luis was the desire to find a circle of friends with whom he could do things after school. Matthew, Manuel, and Jesse usually went home when classes were dismissed and thus in no way filled this need. Though he probably could not have put it into words just yet, Luis would have been quite happy to join a "gang."

In the 1950's, "gangs" were a fact of life in most Hispanic neighborhoods. There were also rivalries between the gangs from various parts of the city and these rivalries simmered steadily and erupted periodically into violence. At the same time, these groups of boys hardly ever had a formal structure. Leadership was chiefly a matter of naturally forceful personalities exerting their will over more pliable individuals. But for the Latino youth, acceptance into any circle of this kind was a gratifying achievement along the road to manhood.

One gang which Luis knew well was a collection of toughs known as the *Dozena Cochina* — the "Dirty Dozen." True to the name, there were exactly a dozen boys affiliated with this freewheeling crew, and one of its central figures was the son of a *compadre* of Luis's father. This streetwise youth, Fernando Cantrell, was older than Luis by several years. But due to the

relationship between their fathers, he fancied himself a kind
of mentor to the younger boy, whom he liked to call his
"cousin."

Once Luis was in the company of an acquaintance named
Benito Herrera. After consuming some food at the Here 'Tis
hamburger place at Swiss and Hall, the two boys got into an
argument outside and began to scuffle. Suddenly a black
Plymouth packed with youths pulled up at the curb and
Fernando Cantrell jumped out.

"What's going on?" he inquired in a peremptory tone of
voice.

"Nothing," both boys assured him.

"Yes, there is! What are you fighting about?"

"It's none of your business," Luis replied pluckily.

"Jump on him again," Fernando ordered, without probing
the matter any further.

"I don't want to fight no more," Luis insisted.

"If *you* don't jump on him, *I* will!" Fernando retorted. He
looked like he meant it.

It was evident even to Benito that he would be better off
going another round with Luis. Their fight resumed, and, for
the first time since they had known each other, Luis won a
decisive victory. But if Benito thought that this would spare him
further grief, he was mistaken.

"Jump on him again," Fernando directed when the action
had subsided.

"No, that's enough. I'm quitting!" Luis replied.

But Fernando had a point to make. To the dismay of the
luckless Benito, the bigger boy now took Luis's place and
worked Benito over with impressive precision and efficiency.

With this minor chore completed, Fernando climbed back
into the Plymouth with a warning his victim was not likely to
forget.

"If I ever hear of you jumping on my cousin again, we're
going to get you!"

The other toughs had remained in the car, but their very
presence had been like a brooding threat. The Plymouth's
motor was gunned and the car screeched away down the

street. The *Dozena Cochina* had done their good deed for the day!

Luis and Benito resumed their business together and continued to be friends. But they never fought each other again!

Violence, or the threat of it, was a way of life among Hispanic gangs. This was especially true whenever there was a dance somewhere, because wherever there was dancing there was also beer. And beer quickly fueled the flames of hostility and aggression and ignited trouble.

Luis and several friends, including his smoking partner, Jesse, dropped in on a dance on one occasion at Exall Park. After a while Fernando and his pack showed up. Whether out of pique or due to his protective instincts toward his "cousin," Fernando ordered Luis to leave. Luis stayed.

But when he and his buddies finally departed, as they made their way down Hall Street toward Swiss Avenue, they sighted the black Plymouth headed their way. They guessed that it was jammed with riders. The entire *Dozena Cochina* often piled into that one vehicle. They could easily pile out as well. And when they did, they enjoyed "whipping up" on their chosen targets.

Luis and his friends took off running.

At the intersection of Hall and Swiss, on the opposite corner from the hamburger place, was a used car lot. The younger boys scooted into this and concealed themselves behind the parked vehicles.

None too soon. As the Plymouth drove by, its occupants fired four or five times in the direction of the cars. Their bullets did not find any human targets, but it was the first time Luis had experienced gunfire aimed in his direction. It was not to be the last.

Little by little, as his childhood slipped by, Luis found himself exposed to both the excitements and the hazards of life as these were generally known to older Hispanic youths. Though he had yet to reach teenage himself, he was rapidly accumulating experiences that conditioned him for a distinctly perilous lifestyle. He was thus caught in the vortex of a way of life that suited the objectives of his supernatural Foe.

At the age of twelve, during his sixth grade year, Luis began hanging around the Alamo School grounds in the afternoon. There he played tag or soccer or whatever else was going on. A group of slightly older boys, who liked to project the image that they were "bad," were often at the playground. As a way of asserting themselves, they took to warning Luis not to be hanging around like that. With language heavily seasoned with curse words and vulgar expressions, they repeatedly threatened to beat him, "stomp" him, or otherwise make him wish he had stayed away.

In this half dozen or so boys there were the makings of a gang which would identify itself with a section of South Dallas called "El Poso." "El Poso" was an area roughly marked off on the south by the Sante Fe railroad tracks, on the west by Good Latimer Expressway, on the east by the old wheat mill, and on the north by the Catholic Church at the corner of Oakland Avenue and Aikens Street.

There was rivalry between "Poso" and the other major area of the neighborhood, called "City." "City" derived its name from its proximity to old City Park and was situated on the other side of Good Latimer.

Luis persisted in coming to the school grounds despite the rough talk for which he was the target. Instinctively he guessed that it was mainly hot air designed to impress him with the gang's authority.

He was partly right. One day the boys lowered the threat level by announcing their intention to remove his pants and hang them on a flagpole. Thereupon the bunch grabbed him and got the trousers off, but they contented themselves with throwing them down in the middle of the school lawn. This done, they walked off to allow their victim to reflect on their toughness.

It proved to be a kind of initiation. Thereafter the group treated Luis in a friendly manner, and within a couple of months Luis could count himself a part of the gang. It was a connection that was going to have tragic consequences.

Luis was soon introduced to vandalism. By placing a small block in the school door, or by leaving a window unlatched, the boys could gain access to Alamo School after dark. Their hope was to find money, though they knew in advance there would be little of that. A normal "take" consisted principally of pencils and paper. Their nighttime visits might have gone almost unnoticed if the boys had not also chosen to ransack some of the classrooms and leave behind them a disordered mess.

Luis was involved in this activity about a half-dozen times. But each time there was fear. This was not a fear of detection, still less was it a fear of God. Instead it was a fear of the dark!

It seemed to Luis and his companions that the long, unlighted corridors of that sprawling, empty structure provided countless hiding places for shadowy figures who might leap out at any moment. As a result, whatever the boys did inside the school they did quickly and then beat a hasty retreat.

School officials regularly summoned the police to report the damage the vandals had done, but their identity was never discovered. Meanwhile, Luis and his friends were branching out into new forms of lawbreaking.

Luis never forgot the first time he and his buddies stripped a stolen bicycle in the alley that ran between Hickory and Dawson Streets. This time the fear of police detection was real and vivid to him, but nothing happened. Eventually Luis's own bicycle was mostly a collage of stolen parts covering a frame that had been rescued from a neighborhood junkyard.

There were other opportunities for petty larceny as well. A couple of blocks from Hall Street, on Cadiz, there was a Nabisco Company warehouse where old cookies were stacked on the rear docks in racks. At first the boys would ask for the cookies, and a few times they got some. But after a while they were told to stop asking, and this command produced a predictable result. They began to steal them.

Covert operations were now "old hat" for this bunch. It was almost ridiculously easy to sneak into the loading area between the trucks and to wait for all the employees to go inside the warehouse. When the coast was clear, the boys would scramble up onto the platform and make off with four or five boxes.

They could be generous or stingy with their loot as the mood happened to strike them. "Want some cookies?" they sometimes asked after they got back to the Alamo School grounds.

When the other kids expressed their eagerness, the boys would say, "Here, have some!" Then they would throw the cookies like missiles in the direction of their schoolmates.

But later they might actually give them some as a gesture of elegant generosity.

In what might have seemed a puzzle to the uninformed observer, Luis continued to attend services at the little church. The church had by now vacated the old clapboard building and was meeting in a former washateria at the corner of Hickory and Jeffries Streets. Despite the downward spiral in his lifestyle, Luis still felt the pull of the atmosphere where he had first met God.

Once a year Luis enjoyed a brief escape from the world of the barrio where he was growing up. Cedar Hill Bible Camp was located on the southwestern fringes of metropolitan Dallas. Through the generosity of the people at his church, Luis was able to attend this camp for a week each summer. The days spent in this wholesome atmosphere of recreation and Christian fellowship furnished Luis with many of his most treasured memories.

The week at camp normally concluded on Friday night with a campfire and testimonies from the various campers and counselors. More than once on such occasions, Luis had risen to his feet and in the flickering glow of the flames told the simple story of how he had received eternal life back at the clapboard church. At such moments, it was almost as if the barrio did not exist at all.

But it did. And Luis could not avoid bringing some of it with him to camp.

One summer during his week at Cedar Hill, Luis had noticed a wristwatch belonging to another boy lying beside the swimming pool while its owner swam. As secretly as possible, Luis picked it up and stuck it into his pocket. Then he made his way to the rear of the cabin to which he was assigned and dug a small hole in the ground. There he buried the stolen watch, wrapped in a handkerchief, so that it could be retrieved when he left for home.

At the next meeting on the camp schedule, an announcement was made that a wristwatch had been taken. The guarantee was given that if the person who took it would bring it back, no questions would be asked. This same announcement was repeated regularly for the rest of the week.

But Luis had no intention of returning a piece of stolen property. Such an action was utterly foreign to the code by which he was growing up.

At week's end Luis made his way to the spot where he had buried the watch. He was stunned to find it gone!

They know! he thought. *Someone saw me!*

His embarrassment was real, but neither then nor in any succeeding year at the camp was anything ever said to him about the incident. It was an experience he never forgot. And like so much else in his contacts with other Christians, it was unique.

Back on the streets of South Dallas, far from the influences that he felt at Cedar Hill, Luis's life would return to its normal pattern. His Father in heaven could not have been pleased with that, but then the Bible had never said that God's children were perfect. If King David could commit adultery and murder, and wise Solomon turn to idolatry in his declining years, was it so strange that a young boy like Luis could steal?

But even though he did steal, his relationship to his divine Parent was as permanent as his relationship to his earthly ones. He had the Bible's word for that, for "the gifts and calling of God are irrevocable."

Nevertheless, the attack of his Enemy had only just begun.

6
The Trap Closes

Luis's family no longer lived on Floyd Street, and Luis had
lost interest in the "jungle" where he had played hooky and
learned to smoke. A succession of residences in the neighborhood known as "El Poso" tied his experience to a different kind
of "jungle." Like the man who had followed his shadowy
companion deep into the woods in search of a dance, Luis was
treading a path that would lead him into a forest of evils.

From there it would be hard indeed for him to find his way
home.

In process of time, the gang to which Luis belonged had its
attention drawn to a car lot located on Jeffries Street. Packed
with brand new Chevrolets, its lure proved irresistible.

A chain-link fence surrounded the lot, but the friends soon
discovered that they could raise it sufficiently at the bottom to
crawl under and get inside. They were delighted to learn that
the cars all had keys in them. This seemed like an invitation too
good to refuse.

On their first few visits, they contented themselves with
gunning the cars forward or backward as space allowed. Then
they made another discovery. The keys to the cars also granted
them access to the spare tires in the trunks.

The gang now went into the business of stealing tires, which they tossed over the fence (or pushed under it) and rolled away. It was not hard to find customers who would pay ten dollars for a new tire, but caution dictated a certain moderation. Over a span of months, therefore, their take probably amounted to no more than a hundred dollars or so.

It was only a matter of time before the obvious next step was taken. The group decided to drive a car off the lot and go riding. The plan was to ram open the gate with one vehicle and then to drive another one away.

Fat Richard made the initial effort to break through the entrance. But Fat Richard had no driving skills at all and was a menace behind a steering wheel. He missed the gate and struck the fence instead, where the car got hopelessly hung up. On a later visit, however, the operation succeeded. The boys managed to get an automobile out of the lot and onto the street.

Then panic took over. The inexperienced car thieves abandoned their stolen vehicle in front of the lot and fled from the scene on foot.

Temporary terror of this kind did nothing to diminish their taste for additional escapades. Police patrols were now more frequent in the vicinity of the lot, but business considerations sent the boys back. Someone they knew was willing to buy a motor if it could be extracted from the right model car. So the gang returned one night, equipped with a pair of pliers, a wrench, and a hammer, determined to accomplish this mission.

The operation failed and the motor remained stubbornly in place. The boys vented their rage by beating it with their tools. Then they fell back on a vandalism that made their activities at Alamo School look pale by comparison.

Enrique, one of the older members of the group, led things off by attacking the windshield of the car they had been working on. Before the gang was through, they had smashed about a half-dozen car windshields and had "flatted" a bevy of tires.

It was their last call on that particular lot, which thereafter was patrolled with special intensity by police squad cars.

But fun was as much the name of the game as money. On warm summer nights, the closed swimming pool on the grounds of Alamo School offered an inviting challenge. Keeping a weather eye out for the park patrol car, the boys would strip down to their underwear, climb the chain-link fence, and dive in.

The park patrolman had been irreverently dubbed "Big Nose Bill." One night he pulled into sight while Luis and his cohorts were enjoying the cooling waters of the pool. A frantic scramble ensued as the half-dozen swimmers clambered hastily over the fence to retrieve their trousers and depart. One of them, a short, slender youth called "Little Lupe," was not quite swift enough and had to scurry up a tree minus his pants. He was trying to hide there inconspicuously as "Big Nose Bill" approached on foot.

"Come down from there!" Bill shouted.

"I can't," Little Lupe pleaded, "I don't have my pants on."

"Well, come down and put them on!" Bill ordered.

What followed was ludicrous to behold. Little Lupe descended from the tree and picked up the one remaining pair of trousers, only to discover that they were Fat Richard's and several sizes too large. Just then Fat Richard, who in his haste had snatched up Lupe's pants, crept back to the scene hoping to retrieve his own. He too was caught. Meanwhile the rest of the swimming party watched from behind the school building with muffled amusement.

"Big Nose Bill" delivered the expected lecture on the evils of trespassing and then let the culprits go. Though he could have turned them over to the juvenile authorities, behind his oversized schnozzle there was a streak of compassion. But the boys were clearly on a collision course with the law which such kindness did nothing to prevent.

Guns naturally held a special fascination for youths like these. Enrique managed to secure a blank gun that sounded like a .22. This led to a stunt that they all regarded as hilariously funny.

A boy named Cesario was another member of their circle. The friends liked to stage their little act in front of a house occupied by Cesario's mother and two sisters. Enrique would fire the blank gun four or five times and Luis, or someone else, would fall to the ground in the frontyard. There he would lie motionless while the rest of the bunch hid. When Cesario's mother and sisters looked outside they would see this apparent victim of gunfire and would frantically call for the police and an ambulance.

By the time either of these arrived, Luis and his buddies would be far away chuckling heartily at the consternation they had caused.

Eventually the boys got their hands on a real .38. The acquisition of this weapon increased their feelings of power, despite the fact that they could not get the gun to fire.

It was about this time that Enrique got involved in a serious argument one night at a local beer joint. The other man was older than Enrique and assaulted him outside the bar with a knife, inflicting several serious wounds. One of these punctured a lung and the teenager was rushed to the hospital in critical condition. Two weeks of uncomfortable recuperation followed. Enrique was lucky to have survived.

The code of the moral "jungle" in which Luis's Enemy stalked him dictated revenge. Luis and Cesario had the .38 in their possession one day underneath the Oakland Street bridge when they caught sight of Enrique's assailant driving leisurely by in his car.

The vehicle could hardly have been going more than 15 miles an hour and its driver furnished a tempting target for Luis, who was holding the gun. He pointed it in the direction of the car, but somehow the impulse to fire was not fulfilled. The automobile passed safely out of range.

In all probability the gun would not have gone off anyway. Originally the gang had thought that the weapon's failure to fire was due to bad bullets. But even with new bullets, the gun continued to malfunction. In what was beyond doubt a piece of completely irrational folly, Luis had actually tested the gun several times with its barrel pointed at his own head, or chest, or stomach! Marks left on the bullet where the firing pin had struck it showed that there had been a measurable impact, but nothing more.

If he had only had the capacity to perceive it, Luis might have sensed the subtle influence of a Power which continually solicited him along the pathway of self-destruction. But a defective .38 was by no means the only route to such a goal.

Luis and two of his brothers, Robert and John (whom everyone called Bobby) were now hawking newspapers on Saturday night in North Dallas. All were stationed at different locations, but Robert worked around Lucas's B & B restaurant, in the area known as Oak Lawn. Robert was small for his age and suffered from a very slight limp due to a bout with rheumatic fever. He managed nevertheless to exaggerate this limp convincingly, and with encouragement from his brothers carried what looked like an excessively heavy load of papers. Regularly Robert could bring in 20 to 25 dollars a night. Luis and Bobby were doing well to bring home ten.

One Saturday night Robert was just outside the Vegas Club. (This was an Oak Lawn night spot owned by Jack Ruby, who later made national news when he gunned down the assassin of John F. Kennedy.) An obviously intoxicated sailor emerged from the club carrying his money in a billfold hung inside his trousers. As he weaved unsteadily away, the billfold dropped to the sidewalk and Robert picked it up. It contained 250 dollars, which he delightedly showed to Luis. After giving 20 dollars to a buddy who knew about his discovery, Robert pocketed the rest of the cash and discarded the wallet behind the club.

About an hour-and-a-half later, a totally sober sailor returned to the scene to look for the lost billfold. Like dutiful good Samaritans, Robert and Luis assisted him in his search, which of course proved fruitless.

It never occurred to Luis that he had any personal responsibility for the morals of his younger brothers. He was not his brothers' keeper — at least, not in that sense.

But by a kind of strange irony, he did really try to look out for them and it was precisely his misguided efforts to do so that allowed his Adversary to close the trap.

Luis was now approaching his sixteenth birthday. With increasing experience on the streets came increased boldness.

Robert had taken a weeklong paper route in which he was assisted by Raymond, another of Luis's younger brothers. On Sunday mornings Luis would often provide these siblings with a unique form of assistance as they dispensed the heavy weekend editions. That was how the trouble began.

Directly across the street from old City Park, on the corner of Ervay and Gould, stood Ben Griffen Ford. This used-car lot was not even protected by a fence, and the car keys were left in the ignition. On Saturday night Luis and one or more of his friends often drove one of these cars away. After joyriding around town until they were ready to quit, the friends would turn in for the night and Luis would park the car a couple of blocks from his house.

Early Sunday morning, when Robert and Raymond left for their route, Luis got up and drove after them. The excitement of throwing their papers from a stolen car embellished a dreary routine with a sense of adventure. Luis enjoyed his image as a streetwise elder brother.

For two or three months this practice continued, with a new vehicle provided on every occasion. When the papers were thrown, Luis would usually take the brothers for a spin down highway 75 as far as the little community of Hutchins. The two other Rodriguez brothers, Bobby and Roy, had a route which they did on foot. Luis could not afford to get Robert and Raymond home too far ahead of the other boys without arousing the curiosity of his mother.

When the trip was finished, the stolen vehicle was ditched somewhere and Luis usually went back to bed. Attendance at church was by now a rare event in Luis's life.

One particular Sunday, a panel truck was the means of transportation. An element of added risk spiced up the routine that morning since on the passenger side of the front windshield were the words: "This vehicle to be operated only by Ben Griffen employees." Even a casual observer could not have mistaken the boys for employees at this time of day. It was almost like daring someone to detect them.

Suddenly a police car came into view and pulled abreast of the truck on the driver's side. The beam from a flashlight stabbed into the interior of the stolen vehicle.

In what seemed like a stroke of good fortune, Raymond had just returned from depositing a paper at a customer's front door. As he slid into the truck on the passenger side, he shrewdly placed his arm on the dashboard so that it blocked any view of the words on the windshield.

"What are you boys doing?" an officer inquired.

"We're just throwing papers, sir," Luis and Robert assured him in a deferential tone of voice. But their hearts were in their throats.

"Okay, then. We'll be seeing you. You all be careful now."

With that the squad car pulled away. The officers had evidently observed Raymond in the act of delivering a paper, but they had not noticed the sign on the windshield.

"Boy, that was close!" Robert exclaimed.

"Yeah!" Luis agreed. "I'm sure glad Raymond covered that sign!" Then, with something less than streetwise cool, he added, "Let's hurry up and get out of here!"

The spin down to Hutchins was taken as usual that morning. But it took a while for the scare to wear off. For the next couple of months the route was covered on foot!

Nevertheless, Ben Griffen's lot remained a powerful attraction. A chain had now been stretched across the driveway exits to discourage the further departure of used cars. Keys were no longer left in the ignition, but hidden behind a visor or underneath a seat. But precautions like these were so useless that they only made Luis and his companions chuckle. In due time Luis was once again his brothers' chauffeur on their Sunday-morning rounds.

There didn't seem to be anything unusual about the Oldsmobile which Luis, Cesario, and Little Lupe drove off the lot one Saturday night. How many other stolen Ben Griffen vehicles had preceded this one, Luis would have been at a loss to say.

Everything went well on the Saturday night joyride and again on Sunday morning as the papers were thrown. But after parking the Oldsmobile, Luis generously left the keys in it for Fat Richard. It was a fatal mistake.

Fat Richard had finally learned how to drive a car. This time he didn't run into any fences. Instead he drove the automobile all over town for several days as if he owned it. By Wednesday, Luis and the rest of the gang were warning him that he'd better park it promptly. By this time it was sure to be on the police "hot list."

Richard was not particularly good at taking advice, even though at 17 he ran heightened risks. Seventeen was the watershed age at which youths who were inclined toward theft often manifested a growing caution. If arrested they could be tried as adults and would thus forfeit the greater leniency of the juvenile courts. But Fat Richard elected to play it brave.

And he was caught. That was on Thursday. His bravado melted quickly under official interrogation and the prospect of a prison term. It was hardly surprising that to save his own skin he "ratted" on Luis and named the younger boy as the actual thief.

On Friday, Cesario was with Luis at the Rodriguez residence while Luis's parents were not at home. A car drove up and two men got out and approached the front door. Like all detectives, they were instantly recognizable as such. The two youths exchanged knowing glances.

"Are you ready to go?" Luis asked his companion. Instinct told him what must have happened.

"Yeah." Cesario replied tersely. Both figured they would be in this together.

The boys met the detectives at the door.

"What's your name?" one of them asked, addressing Luis.

"Luis Rodriguez."

"You'll have to come downtown with us. We want to ask you some questions about a stolen car."

Nothing was said to Cesario. Luis climbed into the waiting vehicle and was escorted to the juvenile detention quarters. These were situated on Harry Hines Boulevard, just north of the downtown area. There the men conducted him into a small foyer and sat him down in a chair. Fat Richard was seated across from them.

"Did you steal an Oldsmobile last weekend?" one of the men began.

"I didn't steal nothing!" was Luis's belligerent reply.

"We have a witness who says you did."

"Who's that? Anyway, he's lying."

The interrogator then turned to Fat Richard. "What's this boy's name?"

In a tonelessly hollow voice, Richard responded, "He's Luis Rodriguez."

"Is he the one who stole the Oldsmobile?"

"Yes."

At that, Luis leaped to his feet, fully intending to lunge at his traitorous friend.

"You'd better sit down," one of the detectives warned. "I'll hit you if you don't."

"You can't hit *me!*" Luis retorted defiantly. "I'm a minor!"

"That won't make any difference. I'll hit you anyway."

A shove from the husky officer returned Luis swiftly to his seat.

"Did you steal that car?"

"No! It's his word against mine. He's a liar. I never stole no car."

"We think you did. We're going to have to lock you up."

"I didn't *do* nothing!" Luis protested, but his air of innocence was lost on the two men. Following a simple booking procedure, Luis found himself assigned to a dormitory-style detention area. About a dozen other youths were quartered there.

It proved to be a long and joyless weekend for Luis. By the time his family learned of his arrest, the juvenile offices had closed for the day and would not reopen until Monday. When his mother was finally able to secure his release, a surge of happiness swept over him.

But matters were serious. On two previous occasions in his young life Luis had been taken to juvenile headquarters and interrogated. But both times he had been quickly released. This time the authorities were planning to charge him with car theft. Fat Richard had been spilling everything he knew about Luis's activities at Ben Griffen. The detectives were delighted to clear up so much unfinished business.

In a midweek session with his caseworker, Luis was told that things would go easier for him if he acknowledged any genuine guilt.

"Did you steal that car?" the caseworker inquired frontally.

"Yes, sir, I did." What mattered now was to get off the hook as painlessly as possible. He would fix things with Fat Richard later on.

"All right," said the caseworker. "We'll plead you guilty. You can expect the judge to give you probation. They never send a first offender to Gatesville."

Luis certainly hoped not. The Gatesville correctional school for boys had a somber reputation. There was plenty of traffic between the barrios of Dallas and that institution, and informants who could describe conditions there were easy to find. One thing Luis knew — it was no country club.

The day for his hearing arrived a week or two later. In the company of his mother, Luis sat nervously in the corridor outside the tiny juvenile courtrooms, waiting his turn. If he had known what was transpiring inside, his anxiety would have taken a quantum jump.

The case immediately preceding his own involved another youth whose name happened to be Felix Rodriguez. Like Luis, he was a resident of the "Poso." But Felix was already married and had a child, even though he was only 14 years of age.

"How is it," the judge wanted to know, "that at such a young age you're already married?"

"That," responded Felix arrogantly, "is none of your _____ business!"

"Gatesville!" decreed the judge. "Next case."

The caseworker stuck his head out into the hall. "Luis, you're next." Julia and her son went in.

Luis listened gingerly as an officer of the court read off the charges against him. He was completely unaware, however, that the judge before whom he stood was not at this moment very favorably disposed toward anyone named Rodriguez.

When he had heard the facts, the judge addressed himself to Luis.

"Did you steal the car?"

"Yes, sir."

"Gatesville," said the judge.

Luis looked at his caseworker and the caseworker looked at him. Stunned disbelief registered on both their faces.

The caseworker turned to address the judge. Something like a "but your honor . . ." was forming on his lips.

"Next case!" declared the judge with unmistakable finality.

Outside the courtroom, Luis was led away by an employee of the detention center. Glancing back down the corridor, he could see his mother engaged in earnest conversation with his caseworker. She too was dismayed by the proceedings. But he would not see her again before his transfer to Gatesville. For now, he was returned to the dormitory holding area.

After supper that night at the juvenile facility, there was a special event. A number of the youthful detainees were permitted to stage a kind of talent program, and among the performers was a girl who sang a wistfully plaintive song. The lyrics included a line that Luis always afterward recalled: "I want to be free, like a bird in a tree."

The words moved him. The grim reality of his impending detention at the state school had begun to sink in.

It was customary procedure for those who had been sentenced to Gatesville to be assigned to small, cell-like rooms until time for their transfer. For some reason Luis had not been put into one of these cubicles, but Fat Richard had been. When the talent program had ended and the juvenile inmates were returning to quarters, Fat Richard committed one final act of perfidy. He informed one of the overseers that Luis, and not he, was headed for Gatesville.

"Are you going to Gatesville?" the attendant inquired of Luis.

"Yes," Luis admitted.

"Okay. You'll have to sleep in there," the man instructed him. He indicated the cubicle in which Richard had been staying.

As Luis was led to these new quarters, he felt a fresh wave of resentment against his one-time buddy. He would have dearly loved five minutes alone with Fat Richard!

As it was, he was simply alone. The door closed behind him on a room containing little more than a small bunk bed and a toilet. A single window faced on the southwest and overlooked a view of Stemmons Expressway, which at that time was still under construction.

It was dark outside now. The lights of downtown Dallas could only be seen if one stretched a bit to peer off to the far left. What chiefly met Luis's gaze was the deserted construction site straight ahead, with its half-finished ramps, pillars, and supports.

Gatesville! He would spend nine to twelve months there Luis felt sure. Though juvenile sentences were deliberately open-ended, that was the normal stay at the facility for a crime such as car theft. It seemed like an awfully long time, as a teenager feels time.

Luis felt also the shadow of uncertainty. Survival at Gatesville could tax all the resources and toughness which a youth could muster. What might transpire in a place like that was better left unguessed. The freedoms of home and the warmth of his family seemed immensely desirable just now.

But they also seemed far away. The construction site rose before Luis's eyes like some remote and lonesome outpost. His father and mother could not help him now.

But he had another Father, One he had been neglecting for some time. And *that* Father was not beyond the reach of His child's voice even here, even now.

Luis prayed.

"Father," he began with unstudied simplicity, "I'm going to Gatesville. I may be there a long time and I don't know what's going to happen. I need Your help."

Not long after that, Luis was in bed and sound asleep.

7
Gatesville

The following morning arrived much too early. Luis was awakened before six and hurried into the mess hall at the detention home well ahead of the normal hour for breakfast. In company with three other boys, who were likewise headed for the Gatesville school, he chowed down a single bowl of cold cereal. It was to be his only food until late that day.

After this meager meal, two plainclothes juvenile officers conducted the group to a station wagon outside, and the boys were told to occupy the rear seats. The officers sat in front.

The youths were not handcuffed. But as the journey commenced, the officer who was riding "shotgun" pulled out his pistol and displayed it ostentatiously.

"On our way down," he began, "if you feel like jumping out of the car, be my guest. We'll be traveling at 70 miles an hour and we won't even slow down to watch you go. I won't even draw my gun. But if any of you guys try to touch the driver, I'll blow your head off!"

If the young prisoners harbored any inclination to attempt an escape, this little speech effectively chilled it. The more than 100-mile trip was completed without a hitch.

Gatesville was a tiny Texas town about 40 miles west of Waco, which in turn was some 90 miles south of metropolitan Dallas. There were scores of towns like it throughout the state. Whatever Gatesville's claims to distinction might have been, the correctional facility was not one of them.

The school for delinquent boys was a large complex of buildings and open fields which occupied land on both sides of the road. On the west lay the facilities to which black youths were assigned, and to the east those which housed Anglo and Hispanic offenders. A relatively low wall of reddish stone was the only physical barrier between the grounds and the highway.

The station wagon drove through an entrance and stopped before a building which stood on the upper curve of an oval-shaped driveway.

The structure turned out to be a dormitory for "freshfish." "Freshfish" was the name universally employed by the inmates of Gatesville to describe those who had newly arrived. It was a designation that only dropped away when a boy was assigned to his permanent quarters.

For a week or so Luis and his companions would be "freshfish." It was not long before they learned that they had entered treacherous waters swarming with predators.

The man into whose charge the officers committed the four boys led them upstairs to survey the facilities. What met Luis's eyes there could hardly have been viewed without a twinge of dismay.

At the top, the stairway opened onto a narrow landing. On either side of the landing and stretching about half the length of the building were two sleeping areas which could only be properly described as cages. Beyond thick wire screens (which reached from ceiling to floor in front of both of these areas) Luis could see in each of them two rows of bunks positioned close together. The bunks were divided by a central aisle that ran the length of the enclosure. Within each of the cages, at one end, stood open stalls which were used for showers.

The remainder of this upper floor was occupied mainly by a large lounge containing chairs and a television set, and by restroom facilities. During the day, the lounge could be frequented at will. At night the boys were locked in the cages. To Luis that was a particularly grim thought.

Little transpired for the remainder of the day. Since lunch had been missed, Luis was famished by the time the "fresh-fish" were lined up and marched off to eat supper. From the moment the station wagon had driven onto the grounds, just as the midday meal hour was ending, Luis had been struck by the large numbers of boys he had seen. They seemed to be everywhere, walking around on the grounds or milling about in front of the various dormitories. *Where did they all come from?* he had wondered. Now on his way to and from the evening meal, the impression was reinforced. Clearly the population at the Gatesville school was substantial, but the degree to which the institution was also infested with evils had yet to unfold.

Luis slept soundly that night. He was quite unaware of the fact that his bunk was situated in an unfortunate location. It was the first bed just inside the door of the cage to which he had been assigned. All seemed to go well until a guard came through the entrance at 5 A.M., well before the rising time to which Luis was generally accustomed. He was still submerged in deep slumber.

But that ended suddenly when he felt a foot in the stomach, followed by a kick in the back, a couple of blows to his bottom, and a fist in his face!

Startled into abrupt wakefulness, Luis quickly perceived that he was expected to get up and dress. He did so with what seemed to him like a single motion. In a few seconds he was standing fully clothed beside his bunk!

The experience had the desired effect. On succeeding mornings he slept more lightly and was readily aroused by the guard's approaching footfalls or by the jangle of the keys with which he unlocked the cage. His preparedness in the following days occasionally brought a faint smile to the guard's hard-bitten countenance.

Tenderness was a commodity in short supply at the Gates-ville school. An orientation lecture during those opening days made that fact abundantly plain. The lecturer minced no words.

"Listen up, you punks!" he began caustically. "You're down here because you're criminals. You've stolen a car or maybe some tires or you've done something else illegal. But around here we've got rules and you'd better get used to them. I'm only going to go over them once, and if I miss anything and you break the rule, you're still to blame. And if you ever get the bright idea you can get away from here, forget about it. Nobody gets away from here and there are three graves out behind the fields of punks who thought they could. So if you 'run,' you'll be caught. We got dogs that will track you down, and after we catch up with you, you'll get a beating you won't forget and you'll do time in the lockup."

The lockup, as it turned out, was a special facility with individual cells where rebellious inmates were consigned for punishment. While being detained there, they were allowed only a half-hour per day outside their cell. It was the kind of experience that Luis devoutly hoped he could avoid.

Luis never saw the graves to which the correctional officer referred. But fellow inmates who had worked far out in the fields assured him they were there. It was a grisly thought.

But sharp blows and rough words were not the only painful aspects of these initial days. There was also the ordeal of the clinic.

The clinic was located on the ground floor of the "freshfish" dormitory. The new arrivals were stripped to the waist and lined up in a circle around the room. At one point along the route, each boy would pass between a doctor and a nurse. The doctor would give him a shot in one arm, and the nurse a shot in the other. When everyone in the circle had passed by them once, both would select new vaccines and the process would begin again. In all, the "freshfish" were favored with somewhere around ten inoculations.

It was too much for some of the youths. More than a few of them passed out before they had completed the cycle. Luis managed to survive without fainting, but wondered how.

On his way back and forth from meals Luis was sometimes greeted by other inmates in a manner he did not at first understand.

"Let me go with your wallet," Chelo Peredes told him one day. Chelo was also from Dallas and had been at the institution six months.

"Let me go with your shoes," another boy would say. Or, "Let me go with your shirt."

Luis was soon to learn that requests like these were in fact demands for the items which were named. If a youth had spent at least six months at the facility, the unwritten code of the place entitled him to acquire whatever he pleased from those who had newly arrived. Failure to surrender the article in question could result in a beating by other inmates. Once he was released from the "freshtank" dormitory, Luis lost all the possessions he had come with.

After the orientation period had ended, Luis was assigned to C Company. On the north side of the central driveway stood four buildings. They were situated on a rise which was referred to as "the hill." The one nearest the front of the grounds was A Company dormitory. A Company was composed of the biggest boys at the institution, irrespective of age, for at Gatesville the prisoners were segregated by size. It was obviously unwise to house the sharks with the minnows!

Next to the A Company dorm stood the main office building, in which there was also a lounge where inmates came when they had visitors from home. Adjacent to this was the B Company dormitory, followed in order by the quarters for C Company and the quarters for D Company. Beyond these four structures, lying somewhat to the northeast of the driveway, were several other dormitories where much smaller boys were housed. In all, the institution at this time sheltered about 1500 youthful offenders.

Luis was 16 now, medium in height and of slender build. He was appropriately placed in a company ranking third in order of size. At the time of the transfer, the "freshtank" graduates were each issued a pair of brogan boots, some khaki pants, and a shirt. From this point on, their "education" would commence in earnest.

If the "freshfish" experience had taught the new inmates the rules, their experience in the company taught them how to survive. The first step was to "wise up."

"Wising up," or *alivianar* as it was called in Spanish, was a process that demanded mastery of an intricate, and often obscene, system of jargon through which various kinds of communication took place. As custom demanded, a knowledgeable member of C Company took it upon himself to "wise up" Luis.

Two weeks were allowed for this instructional process to take hold. Beyond these limits of toleration, a youth who refused to "wise up" was viewed as a "punk," a designation heavy with unfavorable sexual connotations.

So Luis learned to thread the convoluted maze of conduct and conversation by which the internal "system" at Gatesville was controlled. Though formal authority over the institution resided in the hands of its official supervisors, beneath the surface lay a complex code of behavior that dominated inmate life as rigidly as did the rules learned in the "freshtank." And one of the primary requirements of the code was that an inmate always accepted any invitation to fight. To do otherwise was to invite abuse of every kind.

It was therefore no surprise that on one of his first days in the dormitory of Company C Luis was invited by another boy to "get it on." They were in the washroom at the time and they promptly exchanged a few blows. In such encounters anything was legal — hands, feet, or some accessible blunt instrument. At times the instruments were not blunt, but sharp.

A day or so later Mr. Smith, who functioned as the daytime dormitory house father, instructed Luis to put out some trash. To do this Luis had to walk to the rear of the building that housed the mess hall and kitchen, where the trash-dump site was located. As he passed the back of the building, a small knot of boys was loitering there and one of them began to "come on" with the standard inmate lingo. Luis was not yet thoroughly "wised up," but he responded in kind with as much of the jargon as he already knew.

After depositing the trash, Luis headed back past the same group of youths.

"Hey, freshfish," one of the them called out, "let's get it on."

"That's fine by me," Luis responded. "Where? Right here?"

The whole exchange, like all conversation between the Latino inmates, was carried on in Spanish.

"No, not here," the boy replied. "They'll catch us. Let's go in there." He indicated a screened porch area belonging to the kitchen and serving as a kind of storage facility.

"Okay, let's go." Luis followed him to the other end of the building's back side, and both entered the screened porch.

Facing each other now, his prospective opponent edged away from him as Luis watched alertly for his first move. Luis was standing just inside the entrance when suddenly he felt himself shoved into one corner.

Turning swiftly, he faced his new adversary. He was a slightly shorter youth with a husky build and a somewhat roundish face.

"I'm Placido," the boy announced. "I'm from North Dallas."

"Big deal!" Luis rejoined sarcastically.

North Dallas constituted one of the three major barrios of the city along with West Dallas and South Dallas. Though the South Dallas neighborhood was a composite of "El Poso" and "City," the superficial rivalry between these two districts was readily submerged to confront any challenge from some other part of town. Bad blood between North and South Dallas had long been accepted as a basic fact of life.

"I've got a score to settle with you," Placido continued.

"Oh yeah? What's that?"

"Some guys from City who used to be down here did me wrong. I'm going to get even for what they did and you're going to be the one."

"Well, let's get at it right now," Luis suggested, putting a hard edge in his voice.

"No, not now. Later. I have to get back to my Company. But I'm going to get you and you can count on it!"

"I'm ready whenever you are."

Thereupon the group walked off and no blows were struck. But in Placido Luis now had a genuine enemy at the correctional facility — a tool readily available to his greater Enemy — and this was not the last time he would be heard from.

During the first week in a permanent dormitory, the new arrival was required to carry a special card which needed to be signed each day by whoever supervised him on his chores or by his teacher at school. Luis had a hard time keeping this card in tow.

He lost the first one. Mr. Smith gave him another one, but he lost that one too.

About the middle of the week he was summoned to the office of the superintendent, or warden, of the Gatesville school. This office was a special one, not located in the administrative building just south of the A Company dorm. Instead it was situated on the west front corner of the quarters for Company B. As the top official of the institution, the superintendent was completely unloved and was referred to by inmates as "the pig of the hill," an expression which in Spanish was particularly vulgar.

When Luis walked into this office, he was seriously shaken to find four or five guards standing around as the warden sat at his desk. Even at this early stage of his Gatesville experience, Luis was thoroughly aware that the guards frequently ganged up on disobedient youths to administer a painful disciplinary beating. Their chief weapon for such attacks were the heavy, sharp-toed cowboy boots worn by virtually all of them.

Luis sensed uncomfortably that an assault of this kind was in store for him. But he wondered what it could be for.

"Where's your card?" the warden commenced.

"I don't know, sir. I lost it."

"Where?"

"I don't know."

"Here it is," the warden replied, holding it up. "It came to me from the laundry. They found it in a pair of your trousers."

"I'm sorry."

"You'd better be," and with that the man dressed Luis down in harsh language that left little to the imagination.

Then he added, "I want you to learn a lesson."

Here it comes! Luis thought. *They're going to beat me!*

But instead the warden reached into his desk and pulled out another card.

"Take this," he ordered. "But you sure as ____ better not let me find this one somewhere."

"Yes, sir!" Luis responded with a profound sense of relief. He exited the office rapidly.

But he lost that one, too! For some reason Mr. Smith overlooked this negligence and Luis was not reported.

There was something about Mr. Smith that Luis soon came to feel set him apart from most of the other employees of the institution. The streak of visible meanness that was often evident among the supervisory personnel at the facility was not evident in him. Though certainly far from being a "soft touch" — an employee like that could never have made it at Gatesville! — there was in this man what might have been described as a sense of decency.

The same could not be said for "Chuco." "Chuco" was short for *pachuco*, a slang word designating someone who was "hip" or "with it." This man served as the daytime supervisor at C Company on Mr. Smith's day off. He was a different order of personality altogether, and particularly fancied himself a fast draw with the knife he invariably carried in his hip pocket. Luis soon had a chance to observe his little act.

"Swing at me," Chuco would invite some youth who happened to be in the dormitory lounge at the time.

"No, I don't want to," was a standard reply.

"I said, 'swing at me'! You better not get me mad. Go ahead, swing!"

The boy might then aim a halfhearted blow in the guard's direction, whereupon Chuco would whip out his knife in a flash and lay its point up under his victim's chin.

"You better not ever swing at me for real. I can cut your throat in a minute."

With that, Chuco would laugh and put his knife away until he selected a new target.

But there was more than one way of teasing the young residents of Gatesville. It did not go unnoticed that the wives of employees who happened to be visiting Mrs. Smith in the lounge were often attired in low-cut blouses and short skirts.

Dressed in this way, they often managed to sit or move in ways calculated to attract plenty of stares.

Some of these women lived with their husbands in homes situated along the road that led from D Company dormitory to the barn far back on the grounds. From the rear of the kitchen one could look up that road and occasionally see a young inmate dart off the path and go into one of the houses. Naturally there were plenty of stories about the things that transpired inside while husbands were on duty.

Among the more ruthless members of the correctional staff was a one-armed man whom the Hispanic boys called "Manos." The name dripped with irony, since *manos* meant "hands." But "Manos" had only one.

The story that circulated about Manos at the facility was to the effect that he and a black man had each bet their "right arm" in a poker game one time and that Manos had lost the game. His opponent had extracted his pound of flesh by shooting off Manos's right arm with a shotgun.

Whether the story was true or not, it was indisputable that Manos now hated blacks and frequently vented his animosity toward them with unfeeling brutality. At a later period in his stay, Luis witnessed one of these orgies of viciousness. It left him with a vividly repugnant recollection.

Luis and a number of other boys were working that day under Manos's supervision and were repairing a fence on the west side of the oval driveway. On this side of the drive lay the baseball diamond, and south of that the gymnasium. Black youths, whose dormitory facilities were located on the other side of the highway, had access to the gym at specified times. A line of them had just crossed the road and were filing up the driveway in that direction.

"Get that nigger," Manos shouted abruptly, pointing the heavy walking stick which he carried in the direction of the youth he had in mind. No one had ever deciphered the method by which he selected his intended victims. But it was well known that if the victim was not caught the failure would be severely repaid.

Several boys started off after the young black, who knew only too well what was in store for him. He tried to elude them by dashing off onto the baseball diamond, but his flight proved futile. He was literally dragged by his arms and legs into the presence of Manos and dumped unceremoniously at his feet.

What happened next was nauseating to behold. Wielding his thick cane as a cudgel, Manos delivered a series of heavy blows to the figure below him. Each time the youth tried to rise, he would be beaten to the ground anew by a fresh stroke of the stick.

When his venom had dissipated, Manos permitted the youth to leave. Work was resumed on the fence as though nothing had occurred to interrupt it. Whatever the inner demon was that drove him, for the moment it had been exorcised.

It was not hard to believe in Satan in a place like Gatesville. The sheer depravity of its atmosphere furnished a continuous demonstration that the reality of evil was more than an appalling fact. It was an insidious influence whose power could not be adequately explained in mere natural terms. In such an environment, the man who did *not* believe in Satan was a fool!

Perversion was equally a part of the atmosphere of Gatesville. Both seduction and forcible rape might be used on those youths who managed to earn the contempt of their fellow offenders and thus gain the status of "punks." It was a side of life at the school which Luis abhorred intensely and avoided completely. Fortunately there were other ways to fill one's time.

The regimen of the institution required both schooling and a job. In the process of obtaining a job, Luis also acquired another enemy.

During his first week in C Company, Luis spent part of one day out in the fields. These were situated in the southwestern region of the extensive grounds and constituted an assignment wanted by no one. On yet another day, he found himself in a crew detailed to trim grass in front of the dormitory. But since this chore was accomplished by hand, as a line of boys moved slowly over the ground on their knees, it was a task equally uninspiring. Luis began to long for some regular assignment that would be distinctly less grueling.

The opportunity presented itself before the week had end-

ed. Mr. Tucker, who supervised the kitchen, came over to C
Company in need of one helper. When the proposition was
made to the boys gathered in the lounge, Luis volunteered. But
so did a boy named Joaquin, who had been at the facility longer
than Luis. It did not occur to Luis to defer to Joaquin's
institutional seniority.

Mr. Smith chose Luis. The probable reason for this was that
Joaquin had established himself as a troublemaker who was
compelled to take frequent trips to the lockup. The likelihood
that he would hold down any assignment for very long before
requiring this special punishment was notably slim. But
Joaquin did not appreciate being passed over.

That evening, as Luis was whiling away some time in the
Company lounge, Joaquin approached him.

"You bucked me," the youth complained in a surly tone of
voice.

"I needed a job, man," Luis replied.

"If you know what's good for you, you'll quit," Joaquin
retorted with an obvious effort to sound menacing.

Luis ignored that and continued with what he was doing.
Joaquin walked off, but the embers of inward animosity had
been stoked by the incident. They would flare up vigorously
before Luis again saw freedom.

Of course Luis kept his job in the kitchen. Responsiveness to
pressure was not one of his virtues, as Miss Nichols of Stephen
F. Austin school (and a host of others) could have told Joaquin.
But the assignment was just what Luis had hoped for, even if
it did require rising at 3:30 A.M. He made up his mind to hang
onto it.

Luis's daily program was now established. The night guard
awakened him at the wee hour his job necessitated. Luis would
then make his way to the kitchen, while it was still dark, to help
prepare breakfast. His tasks there would normally be finished
around 9 o'clock. Thereafter an idle hour or so could be spent
at Company C watching television or chatting with Mr. Smith.
Most of the boys were elsewhere at this time of the morning.
Then came the lunch shift and the end of his kitchen chores for
that day. In the afternoon there was school, and in the evening
dinner and a couple more hours in the dormitory lounge,

where Luis often played cards. About 9 o'clock the boys were herded upstairs, allowed to shower, and locked in the cages where they slept. It was a pattern that was to become routinely familiar in the months that lay ahead.

But there were advantages to kitchen labor which Luis did not immediately suspect. For one thing, Mr. Tucker proved himself to be among Gatesville's more reasonable employees, a breed not easy to encounter there. For another thing, there was opportunity to acquire the respect of Company A.

This magisterial collection of youths, composed as it was of the biggest boys at the facility, "ran the hill." This was simply a way of saying that they enforced the internal system governing inmate life. When word "came down" from A Company that such and such a thing was to be done (or not to be done) this command was ignored by the lesser companies only at their peril. And among the prerogatives exercised by Company A was the right to call for a "Geronimo."

A "Geronimo," Luis had heard, was about as wild a scene as Gatesville could witness. Since the mess hall could not accommodate the entire institutional population all at one time, the boys ate in stages and A Company always ate first. After they left, if they had given the indication, the other boys in the dining area would know the exact minute at which the action was to begin.

When that moment struck, pandemonium would break loose. Chairs and tables would be overturned, trays and dishes would be hurled in every direction, windows would be smashed, and there would be a general stampede for any available exit. Meanwhile, the boys in A Company who were poised in readiness back at their dormitory would take advantage of the clamor and confusion to make a break for freedom.

It was rare that such breakouts had any success at all. The personnel at the institution were nearly as proficient in rounding up runaways as they bragged of being. Few of the boys who chose to "run" ran very far. Still, it gave a youth some feeling of *machismo* to be able to come back boasting, "I was a free man for five hours," or however long he had actually avoided recapture.

Luis was never to actually see a "Geronimo," but the

authority of A Company was a reality that touched him in more than one way. He soon learned that among his kitchen duties was the requirement that the boys from that dormitory be treated to special culinary considerations. At breakfast, they alone were served toast buttered on both sides. And though the yolks were normally broken in any batch of eggs that was hard-fried, eggs for Company A were accorded special care. They were also duly complemented by the largest available strips of bacon.

At lunch similar amenities were provided. If sandwiches were on tap, double meat and extra lettuce and mayonnaise were in order. If Swiss steak happened to be on the menu, cuts specially spiced up were prepared for the "kings of the hill."

But it was an art that took a little skill to master to see that these favors were properly distributed. This was due to the fact that life at Gatesville was carefully segregated by long-standing inmate practice, so that Hispanics mingled only with Hispanics and Anglos with Anglos. On any given occasion when the members of a particular company were using the dormitory lounge, one could always observe the Hispanic youths at one end and the Anglo boys at the other. It followed from this that Hispanics who labored in the kitchen prepared and served their special treats only to the Hispanic members of Company A. The Anglo help did a similar service to their own kind.

It would have helped to implement such conventions if the Anglos and Hispanics had also been segregated as they passed through the cafeteria line. But the supervisory personnel failed to cooperate on that. Instead they insisted that the two races alternate in the line and sit three and three at each table. It was therefore necessary for new help like Luis to learn how to "set up" so that he and his Latino co-workers could serve their specialties only to fellow Latinos.

But Luis mastered the somewhat intricate procedure rapidly. He soon became a familiar face to the A Company members who benefited from his daily largess. Although he did not know it at the time, it was well that he had acquired the chance to store up some goodwill among this autocratic circle of boys. Before his sojourn at Gatesville was over, he would need it.

8
His Father's Rod

They called it "beat the devil." And there were few leisure activities more popular among the inmates at Gatesville than this one. Actually it was a card game, a special form of solitaire that was played over and over again.

Luis loved it. The player dealt 52 cards facedown into 13 piles, each of which was a stack of four. Starting with the thirteenth stack, he would turn over one card. Its number would signal the pile from which he would draw next, or, if it were a Jack, Queen, or King, he would pull from the eleventh, twelfth, or final stack respectively. The object of the game was to pick up all the cards before drawing the four Kings. If that feat were accomplished, the devil was beaten.

During his time at the correctional facility, Luis occupied more hours than he could count in this absorbing diversion. It would have been no exaggeration to say that he had tried to "beat the devil" somewhere between 200 and 300 times. He never did it once!

There was an undetected irony in that. For as surely as his leisure hours failed to register a victory over his "opponent," a comparable failure beset his life. In fact, his very presence at the Gatesville school represented a significant defeat at the hand of his Enemy, whose prolonged assault on Luis's conduct and morals had now borne such bitter fruit.

Still, something was happening to Luis here that was genuinely new. On his very first Sunday at the institution, while he was still in the "freshtank," Luis had chosen to attend services at the Protestant chapel rather than the Catholic one. This was far from the natural thing to do in the light of the sharp division at the facility between the Hispanic and Anglo inmates. It was nothing short of remarkable that in this respect alone Luis consciously chose a course that diverged from that of his fellow Latinos.

Of course, in the outside world it was an unjustified stereotype to view all Hispanics as though they belonged to a single religion. Such a perception of them was not only inaccurate, but one which they often quite rightly resented. But within the confines of the correctional facility, this stereotype was a functional reality, a part of the elaborate code which determined the lifestyle of the youthful inhabitants. By long-standing convention, Hispanic boys attended Catholic services.

One day, at Company C, during the midmorning break in his shifts at the kitchen, Luis was called on by the Protestant chaplain.

"I want to invite you to come back to our services," he said cordially. "I understand you are not Catholic."

"That's right, I'm not," Luis replied. "But I work in the kitchen now and I work on Sundays while church is going on. That's why I haven't been coming."

"Well, if you ever get the chance, we'll be glad to see you. I wanted you to know you are welcome."

"Thank you, sir. I'm glad you came over."

Luis *was* glad the man had come. More than ever there existed in Luis a spiritual consciousness which had been forged by his experiences at the clapboard church. With increasing distinctness, he was aware of a religious identity which distinguished him from the Hispanic youths with whom he associated day by day. In particular, there were none of them whom he had much reason to believe possessed eternal life. But on the other hand they had no particular reason to guess this about him either.

That was true even of Juanio, Huero, and Fred, with whom he eventually struck up a close relationship. It was not the first foursome Luis had been involved with in his life, but it was a far cry from the old consortium with Manuel, Matthew, and Jesse. Juanio was from San Antonio (a fact that was soon to prove troublesome), and he was an easygoing type who liked to joke. Huero, short and rather quiet, was from Victoria, down in the valley. Fred was about Huero's size, from Dallas, and, like Juanio, he was fun to be with.

But the quartet's idea of a good time was not mischief, but an evening of cards. There were many such evenings after their friendship began to form somewhere around the second month of Luis's stay at Gatesville. Unlike the troublemakers who had coalesced into the group to which Joaquin belonged, these four youths preferred to do "good time" and make their stay at the facility as short as possible.

Their association, however, was not destined to last.

Among the Hispanic residents of Gatesville there were two long-established factions. In the event of trouble, every Latino youth either "jumped for" Houston or "jumped for" San Antonio. This familiar inmate jargon was the standard way of stating whose side you were on in the event of a general brawl or some other form of factional tension. Like everything else that the internal system decreed, it was a carefully orchestrated arrangement.

Dallas always "jumped for" Houston, and these two cities formed the bulk of one of the rival groups. Victoria, from which Huero came, fell under this particular umbrella by virtue of its proximity to Houston. On the other hand, places like Waco and El Paso belonged in the orbit of San Antonio. In this way, the two largest metropolitan sources of Latino delinquents formed the centers around which were clustered the various satellite towns. The upshot of this apportionment was an approximate equalization of forces. Since Dallas also was a sizable city, its alliance with Houston was balanced by a somewhat larger number of medium-sized allies for San Antonio.

A kind of fairness thus prevailed. A considerable advantage accrued to inmates from small towns since they were afforded the protection of the larger group. But these benefits were not without their price. While a Latino who "jumped for" one group was not restricted from talking to the members of another, tight friendships across these boundaries were strictly forbidden. Juanio now had this fact called to his attention.

He broke the news one day to his three buddies.

"They told me I have to quit hanging around with you guys," he reported with just a trace of dejection. "I jump for San Antonio."

"Okay, we understand," his companions assured him, "but we can still be friends."

"Yeah, but I can't play cards and stuff like that. I've got to stop hanging around."

But he didn't, at least not right away. The lure of the card table was too great, and he joined in one evening for another game.

"I'll see if they do anything," he explained hopefully.

The next time he talked with his friends, he gave a somber report.

"They told me, 'We're not going to tell you again. If you don't quit hanging out like that, we're going to give you Kangaroo Court.' They mean it, too. So I guess I'll have to cut you loose."

"We understand. It's all right," his partners told him. "Guess we'll have to find another fourth."

"Kangaroo Court" was an experience you could never wish on anyone you really thought of as your friend. The victim of this disciplinary procedure was allowed to squat on his haunches, place his head facedown on his knees, clasp his hands behind his neck, and try with his arms to shield his temples, cheeks, and the sides of his body as best he could. Then he was assaulted by a series of vicious kicks from five or six boys whose brogan boots could leave plenty of bruises even on those who effectively protected their most tender points. Naturally, Juanio wanted no part of that.

Juanio drifted out of their circle. It was too bad, but at the same time it was a fact of life. Gatesville was not the place to form lasting friendships, and even Huero and Fred would eventually become little more than memories to Luis.

Yet there was one attachment whose bonds were strengthened by the experience Luis was having. It was a relationship that had existed for some time, but was in urgent need of cultivation. And it was with God.

Luis's mother visited him regularly on Saturdays, accompanied usually by other members of the Rodriguez clan. Her frequent trips were a reminder that he belonged to a home where he was loved, and which he loved in return. Before he fell asleep at night he regularly prayed that God would watch over his family back in Dallas. Simple as this was, it was something he had never done before. He had now opened the lines of communication with his heavenly Father.

There was also a man from the church who usually came down on Mondays. That was Zane, who had known Luis for about three years and who taught the Sunday school class which Luis's four younger brothers attended. The clapboard church, which had previously taken a step up to quarters in a former washateria, was now located in its best facilities ever — an old storefront building directly across the street from the house where Luis's family currently lived.

Before the Monday visit, Luis usually received a letter from Zane asking questions whose answers had to be looked up in a book of the Bible called First Corinthians. Luis could not recall ever opening the Bible anywhere except in church, but now he found himself doing it once or twice a week.

After school, during the free period before supper, was the best time for that. Luis would get back to C Company about 4 o'clock, while most of the rest of the boys did not usually begin to come in until five. With an hour or so of relative quiet available in the dormitory lounge, Luis searched the chapter for that week to discover the answers he would give on the approaching Monday. To his surprise, despite his severely limited reading ability (he had quit school in the ninth grade), Luis found that he could usually dig the information out. And he actually enjoyed doing it!

There were one or two other youths in the company who also read their Bibles at times. And those who did not left alone those who did. Turning to God while in prison was an impulse which all prisoners understood and one which each individual carried out in his own way. If one youth promised to say so many Hail Mary's, another might guarantee his Maker that he would be regular at Mass. But the need for help from a Higher Power was sensed in a tangible way in an institution like this, however often and quickly it might be forgotten on the outside.

But there was more to Luis's experience with the Bible than that. Somehow he found this study sharpening his awareness that he was genuinely God's child. He already knew that he was, but now the implications of this reality were beginning to dawn on him. His life was not a very good life by the standards of the Bible, though he was well aware that this did not affect the gift of eternal life which he had accepted long ago at the clapboard church. What it did do was make him feel ashamed.

"Help me to be good," was the straightforward request he sometimes now addressed to his heavenly Father as he lay in his bunk at night. "When I get out of here," he might add, "I want to go back to church and learn more."

But getting out was quite another matter. Furthermore, it was hard to be "good" in a place like Gatesville, where there was precious little to encourage it. Without suspecting it, Luis was headed toward his hardest days at the facility.

Joaquin proved to be a continuing thorn in Luis's side. He did not like Luis and made no attempt to conceal it. He was especially pointed in deriding Luis because of the visitor he had each Monday. In the "wised-up" lingo of the institution, he suggested a vulgar explanation for these visits which Luis did not appreciate.

There were times that Luis wished Zane would stay at home. The other residents of C dormitory could not comprehend the interest this Anglo showed in Luis and were stubbornly impervious to all efforts to explain it. But Joaquin was particuarly obnoxious.

Luis challenged him a few times to "get it on," but Joaquin preferred to fight through surrogates. Despite the bold front he put on, he had no taste for actual combat. His favorite substitute was a powerful hulk of a youth called Oscar.

How Oscar had wound up in Company C Luis could never understand. His size and bulk seemed to qualify him for A Company or at the very least B Company. But here he was in C Company and a staunch ally of Joaquin at that. Luis had exchanged punches with him more than once, and the sting from Oscar's heavy blows did not quickly wear off.

And then it happened. Trouble erupted which at first had nothing to do with Company C or with Oscar and Joaquin. But it triggered one of the most harrowing weeks Luis had ever experienced in his entire youthful life.

Cirilo was a boy from South Dallas who was younger than Luis. One day he was attacked by several inmates who hailed from North Dallas, among whom was a buddy of Placido's named Miguel. Cirilo was from Company D, and being clearly outsized, he took measures for self-defense in the event of another assault. Taking a long nail which he had picked up somewhere, he flattened its shaft with a hammer so that it served as a tolerable substitute for a knife.

Just as he had anticipated, he was accosted one day by Miguel. In the ensuing encounter Cirilo managed to stab the larger boy seven or eight times. He afterward boasted that the only reason he had stopped when he did was that on his final thrust he had been unable to extract the weapon from his opponent's body.

Miguel was taken to the infirmary for treatment and Cirilo was banished to the lockup. The repercussions began quickly.

Unfortunately for Luis, this incident rekindled the simmering rivalry that always existed between North and South Dallas. For purposes of this feud, "El Poso" was not distinguished from "City," and Cirilo was from "City" while Miguel was from North Dallas. It was unthinkable that the wounding of Miguel could go unavenged.

But Cirilo was now out of range in the lockup, so other victims had to be located. The prospects were limited, since at this time Luis was one of only four older youths from South Dallas presently at the institution. One of these was the boy named Chelo Peredes, who had staked claim to Luis's wallet during Luis's early days in the "freshtank." But Chelo had been here about a year and had accumulated enough prestige not to be selected as a target. The same was true of Evodio, whose esteem stood even higher by virtue of his being a Gatesville four-timer.

That left, besides Luis, only Felix Rodriguez. Felix was the youth who had greased Luis's path to the correctional facility by his insolence toward the judge in juvenile court. He had also been one of the boys in the car with Luis on the trip down. Now he was about to make yet another unwitting contribution to Luis's problems.

Word now "came down" that the boys from "City" were to get trouble. In Miguel's buddy Placido, North Dallas had a "big dog" in Company A who could set the wheels in motion. South Dallas, on the other hand, had no residents there or even in Company B. Luis had the misfortune of being the oldest representative of "City" at the facility.

There were no secrets at Gatesville. Felix was soon informed of what lay in store for him, as was Luis. But Felix chose to disengage. He went directly to the warden to report this threat to his health and safety. In the jargon of his peers, he "squealed to the pig of the hill."

The warden could play the game rough as well. The word was now passed that anyone who touched Felix was guaranteed a beating they were not going to enjoy. Since this signified the standard multiple assault by the cowboy-booted guards, it was an effective threat. Felix had acquired physical immunity but at the cost of his status among fellow inmates. It was agreed that if he had squealed once, he would do it again. Felix did not "count" anymore.

That left only Luis! And Luis was not about to squeal. Placido was only too glad for a chance to make Luis's life unhappy.

So was Joaquin, who had always declined any individual encounter with Luis. But with the word now out from A Company, Luis became a legitimate target for group assault. Joaquin rallied his crew to take advantage of the situation.

Luis was on his way to school one afternoon when he sighted Joaquin, Oscar, Sergio, and several other boys collected at one side of the building, obviously awaiting his arrival. It took no gift of prescience to guess what they had in mind.

"We're going to get it on," Joaquin announced as Luis came up to them.

"Okay, I'm ready. Where?" There was no possibility of refusing the engagement, Luis knew, since to do so only multiplied one's problems. If you were not inclined to squeal, you had to face the music.

"Downstairs in the schoolhouse," Joaquin responded.

That did not appeal to Luis. Down there, in the restroom, they would have him alone. The possibility that one of them possessed a knife could not be discounted.

"No, not down there," Luis shot back. "Let's go behind the schoolhouse."

It was a more prudent location, Luis reasoned. Out in the open there was always a chance that some of the supervisory personnel might observe the fight and intervene. A knifing was less probable in such visible circumstances.

"It's not going to be behind the schoolhouse," the youths insisted. "We're going downstairs."

Luis reluctantly agreed. Fortunately he managed to precede them down the stairs and into the washroom. In this way he could face them and have a wall at his back.

When he had assumed this position, the gang advanced on Luis, who quickly dropped into the hunched-down posture used for "Kangaroo Court." For a couple of minutes — which seemed easily many times that long — the half-dozen attackers rained kicks on the exposed portions of his body. One of these blows severely grazed his left cheek.

Then it was over. The boys had slipped away from their duties in the field and could not risk being gone too long. After they departed, Luis got up, washed his face, and went to class. He hurt in a lot of places and would have his share of tender spots for a long time.

When he returned from school that afternoon and entered C dormitory, Mr. Smith noticed the bruise on his cheek.

"What happened, Luis?" the house father wanted to know.

"It's nothing," Luis replied as casually as possible.

"How did you get it?" Mr. Smith persisted with ill-concealed suspicion. When word of trouble "came down" from Company A, it usually reached the supervisors as well. Like every other similar institution, Gatesville had its snitches who curried favor and volunteered information they thought would enhance their standing with those in authority.

"I scraped it against a door," Luis lied.

"Are you sure?"

"Yeah."

The first ordeal had been navigated with only a minimum of physical damage. But Luis knew that his difficulties were not likely to end there, and in this regard he was perfectly correct. Before much time had expired, he was warned that more hazards lay ahead.

A day or so later, Luis had just finished dinner in the mess hall. It was the only meal of the day he ate with the other inmates. He was now passing through the line which filed by the dishwashing area in order to surrender his utensils and tray.

Placido worked on the other side of a counter window through which he collected the trays, scraped them, and then stacked them in racks to be washed by machine. From time to time he had to hold up the line while he replaced a filled rack or got a new garbage can. Much too coincidentally, so it seemed to Luis, he found a reason to halt the line just as Luis was about to hand over his tray.

"I'm going to get you," Placido informed him in a tone resonant with hostility.

"You ain't going to do anything," Luis retorted disdainfully. "You ain't nothing!"

"We're going to get it on," Placido hissed.

"When do you want it?" Luis inquired fiercely. "Tonight?"

"No, I've got to work. But we're going to get it on."

"How about tomorrow morning after our shifts?"

"You got it. Tomorrow morning out back," Placido promised him.

Luis now shoved his tray roughly at the other boy, who snatched it vigorously out of his hand. A guard standing nearby observed them.

"What's going on?" he wanted to know.

"Nothing," Luis replied.

"Nothing," agreed Placido.

It did not seem likely to Luis that Placido would turn up the next morning alone. That was not his style, and another gang assault was a distinct possibility. In fact, Placido did not turn up at all.

Someone else did.

As Luis was winding up his breakfast chores, a larger youth from Company B, who worked in the butcher shop, approached him.

"I want to see you in the john," he announced.

Luis knew what that was about.

"In a couple minutes," he replied. "I have to get away from here."

The boy walked off. Luis was concerned. His prospective opponent might very well turn up armed with a knife from the butcher shop, which could do serious damage. Some kind of defensive measure seemed necessary. He picked up a large serving spoon and stuck it in his back pocket.

Leaving the kitchen, Luis entered a hallway that turned left as it passed the butcher shop and right again in the direction of the restroom. Cautiously he opened the restroom door and entered.

The other youth was already there, facing him. No knife was visible.

"Be cool," his potential adversary advised.

Luis eyed him suspiciously without responding.

"I said, be cool," the boy repeated. "They want me to get it on with you, but I'm not going to fight you."

"How come?" Luis inquired, with his distrust hardly diminished.

"I know some guys from 'City,' " the youth informed him. "I know Mario Mendez and Jaime and Arnulfo. When they were down here they were my friends. They covered for me and backed me up. I owe them something for that. So I'm going to return the favor. I'm not going to fight you."

"That sounds all right," Luis replied, beginning to feel relieved.

"But now you got to do me a favor," the boy continued.

"What's that?" Luis felt his suspicion renewed.

"When you come outa here, you gotta act like we had a fight. Put your hand on your face or something like that. They'll think we got it on and won't ask any questions."

"It's okay by me." That was an understatement.

They stayed in the washroom for a few minutes more, then the larger boy made his exit. After what seemed like an appropriate interval, Luis also left.

As he made his way down the hall past workrooms and the butcher shop itself, any youth who happened to glance up would have noticed his shuffling gait and the hand he held to his head. It was a performance worthy of an academy award! And as far as Luis knew, no one afterward ever suspected that Placido's agent had not fulfilled his assignment.

But the ensuing days brought more ominous threats. Luis might be on his way to the store, or going to and from school, or traveling any other route, when someone would say, "We're going to get you for what happened to Miguel!" Luis wondered if the storm clouds would ever lift before something really serious took place. At night he asked God's help.

He was at the urinal in the dormitory restroom one day when, out of the corner of his eye, he saw Oscar, Joaquin, and their bunch come in. A warning signal flashed through his brain, but before he could react he felt a heavy blow to the rib cage.

Knocked off balance, he instinctively slumped down in "Kangaroo Court" style in between the urinal and a toilet. A flurry of vicious kicks were aimed in his direction, but the facilities on either side of him limited the attackers' ability to land their blows in the usual spots. After a moment or two, the gang withdrew. Commotions like this could not be prolonged without the risk of detection.

Luis got up again and went about the business of the day. He reminded himself that he had better stay alert at all times, especially in restrooms.

This sort of thing might well have gone on indefinitely had it not been for Luis's role in the kitchen. "Luisio," as Company A boys sometimes called him, had served up many a special treat to the kings of the hill. These boys now intervened on his behalf. Word soon "came down" that Luis could no longer be the target for group attacks.

As the institutional grapevine described it to Luis, Company A had pronounced on the matter and had communicated their decision to Placido.

"It's gotta stop now," they informed him. "He's taken his punishment and he hasn't squealed on anybody. It can't just go on like this. If you want something with Luis, you can have him yourself, but don't send anybody else to do it for you."

That dictum applied to everybody, including Joaquin, Oscar, and the rest. A further assault on Luis would now have invited retribution from A Company. This was a consequence that Joaquin and his crew were not prepared to risk. The storm had finally passed.

Though Luis probably could not have brought it to mind, there was a story in the Bible about Moses, whose rod had been transformed into a serpent when he threw it on the ground. When he picked it up again, it was changed back into a rod. There was a symbolism in that which was strikingly pertinent to Luis. What he had just been through, and indeed all of his experience at Gatesville, was like the application of a serpent-rod. From one perspective this experience displayed the bitter hatred of the ancient Serpent himself. From another perspective it reflected the disciplinary rod which the hand of his heavenly Father wielded with perfect control.

Luis was now approaching the end of his first three months at the institution. A hearing would be set to determine the status of his case. By well-established precedent, Luis could expect a virtually automatic extension of his term by an additional six months. And beyond that, a second three months' extension was usual.

On the appointed day Luis was summoned before a review committee, which convened in the administration building. Its members encouraged him to talk.

"Is there any reason why we ought to release you?" one of them inquired.

"Yes, sir," Luis replied, "I've learned my lesson."

"What have you learned?"

"Well, I've learned that I don't want to spend the rest of my life in a place like this having someone tell me what to do."

"Is that all you've learned?"

"I've also learned it don't pay to steal."

"We hope you have."

The committee then informed Luis that they had four letters all recommending he be released.

"Mr. Smith and Mr. Tucker have both written letters for you," they said, "and both of them have given you a good report. They think it would be best to release you."

The other two letters, it turned out, had come from his caseworker at the institution and from Zane.

"This would be a highly unusual release," they insisted. "We just don't do this. Our policy is to give a boy an addtional six months. When he's been here nine months to a year we then give serious consideration to releasing him. But that's providing he has a good record."

Luis knew this, of course, and had anticipated a term of comparable length from the very day he had been sentenced to the facility.

"But perhaps," the committee spokesman continued, "you're a different kind of boy. Your record is clean. You haven't been in a fight and you haven't been reported for stealing anything. You haven't tried to run away and you're not a troublemaker. We don't have any bad reports about you, which is very unusual. It may be best to release you. We'll consider it and let you know."

On that note the hearing was terminated. But a couple of days later, Luis was called in again.

"All right," they said, "you're ready to go. We're going to release you. The only thing we have to do now is send your papers to Austin. It should take two or three weeks to get them back, and after that we'll fix the exact day for you to go home."

The elation Luis felt as he returned to the dormitory was hard to describe, but it was mingled with a new concern. If his fellow inmates learned that he was to obtain his freedom after only a three months' stay at the facility, they would never allow it to happen. They would make trouble. They would force him to fight. And that would be enough. One negative mark added to his record now would dash all hope of immediate release. Suddenly his situation was again fraught with danger.

When he got back to Company C, he was greeted with intense curiosity.

"Hey, what happened? Are they going to cut you loose or what?" his dormmates inquired.

Luis decided to tread this path with care.

"Have you ever heard of anybody being released after three months?" Luis retorted as though the very thought was absurd.

"What did they do to you?" the boys wanted to know. "How many months did they give you?"

"What's the standard procedure?" Luis parried their question with his own.

"Six months," they agreed.

"Well, do you need me to explain this to you?" He hoped it would sound stupid of them to inquire further and that they would take this for an answer.

It worked. The questioning died out and everyone assumed that Luis had been handed the normal six months' extension. Meanwhile, Luis counted the days until his papers would come and kept as low a profile as he possibly could. It was a little like walking on tacks. The slightest eruption of trouble could prove fatal.

Then one day Mr. Smith gave him the news he was waiting for.

"Your papers have come back, Luis," he reported. "You're ready to go. You get out next Tuesday."

"Mr. Smith," Luis requested with deep earnestness, "do you think you could keep this quiet? You know what the boys will do to me if they find out. They'll make me fight and it'll kill my release."

"Okay, Luis, I understand," Mr. Smith said, and he kept his word.

Monday came, and it was the day for Luis to pick up new clothes and bring them to the dormitory so he could wear them home the next morning. But bringing them here would be a clear signal that his release was imminent, and it would escalate his peril sharply. If at all possible he had to get the clothes in unobserved.

Once again, with the aid of Mr. Smith, this was accomplished. The house father turned the clothes over to his wife to put in Luis's locker in the area where personal belongings were stored.

"Put these up," he told her, "and don't let anyone get hold of them until tomorrow morning." By using Mrs. Smith for this purpose, the boys who usually handled storage were bypassed and were none the wiser. So far, so good.

Evening arrived. It was traditional for boys who were going home the next day to be allowed a small party with a few friends. There was a room upstairs where this could be done. For an hour or so past normal bedtime the party goers would sip soft drinks, munch candies, and listen to records or a radio. It was the best way to say a joyful goodbye to Gatesville, and Luis wanted the experience.

When the boys were finally herded upstairs to get ready for bed, Luis approached the guard who was on night duty.

"Hey, I go home tomorrow," he announced in a cautious tone of voice.

"You go *where?*" the night man replied incredulously.

"I'm going home tomorrow," Luis repeated.

"You're going *home?*"

"Yeah. I was wondering if I could have my little party with my friends."

"Luis, you're not going home!" The guard thought he was joking or trying to pull a fast one.

"Yes, I am. My clothes are in my locker. Look in my locker."

The guard went downstairs to the locker room and found Luis's new clothes.

"Okay. They're there all right. You got any stuff for your party?"

Luis had managed to bring in provisions for the occasion, but as he collected his friends the questions started to come.

"Man, you going home?" his dormmates asked with surprise. "You lied to us."

"I didn't lie to you."

"Yes, you did! You said they gave you six months."

"I didn't say they gave me six months," Luis insisted. "I said that's what they *usually* did."

"Aw, man," they complained, "we thought you got six months." They eyed him enviously as he and his companions went off to celebrate.

Everyone was asleep when the party finally ended and Luis and his friends retired to their bunks. *One more night in this cage!* Luis thought to himself. *One more night!* Soon he had drifted into slumber.

When morning came, for once Luis could go to breakfast with everyone else. After that, it would be back to the dormitory to change into his new clothes, then over to the administration building to pick up his release and to board the institutional bus that would take him to town. The bus left at 9 o'clock.

But Luis could tell that Joaquin, Oscar, and Sergio were looking for their chance. They were running their mouths at full speed, "coming on" with the usual inmate lingo and hoping to set the stage for trouble. Luis shot back at them with all the standard responses, but he knew he must confine any confrontation to words alone. Anything more than that, so close to freedom, would be an intolerable disaster.

Mr. Smith was on duty again and Luis managed to follow him around almost everywhere he went. It was a superb imitation of Old Dog Tray, but under the house father's watchful eyes no one would dare to start a fight. They could talk all they wanted to, but talk didn't accomplish anything.

Breakfast passed. When he got back to Company C, Mr. Smith said to him, "All right, Luis. Get your clothes and go upstairs and change." The golden moment had almost arrived.

Luis changed clothes upstairs in the cage area and started down again. The stairway took a right turn at a landing which was about five steps above the hallway on the first floor. Luis reached the landing and made the turn. But a couple of steps further and he stopped abruptly. At the foot of the stairs stood Joaquin, Oscar, and Sergio.

Joaquin, as usual, was spouting a gusher of words, but it was Sergio who started up the steps.

"We're going to get it on," he informed Luis ominously.

"Sergio, I don't want to get it on," Luis rejoined as calmly as he could. But inside he felt the tension rising.

"Man, if you don't get it on with me, you know what's going to happen," Sergio persisted. "I'm going to jump you and all the guys here are going to see you didn't fight back and everybody's going to think you're a punk!"

"Sergio, I don't want to fight, man. I'm going home, man, and I don't want nothing to do with this place *again!*" He stressed this last word instinctively. It was as though two futures now hung in the balance on that staircase.

"We don't have nothing to do with that," Sergio retorted in a tone totally devoid of any sympathy. Then he swung at Luis.

But Luis was a step or two above him and the blow missed. Luis returned it with a sharp kick to Sergio's body, which sent his opponent tumbling backward down the stairs. There he collided with Joaquin and Oscar.

In a flash, Luis was down the stairs and into the hallway. Instinctively he got ready to defend himself.

But Mr. Smith was also in the hall only a few paces away. Attracted by the commotion, he rushed over.

"What's going on?" Mr. Smith demanded.

No one said anything.

"Luis, what's wrong?" Mr. Smith now focused on him.

"Nothing," replied Luis a bit sheepishly.

"What's wrong, Luis?" Mr. Smith repeated emphatically.

"Nothing," Luis insisted.

Then Mr. Smith turned to Sergio, "You fighting, Sergio?"

"No," was the sullen response.

"Luis," said Mr. Smith, "do you want to go home?"

"Yes, sir!" It was now about 8:45.

"You see that front door?" Mr. Smith asked.

"Yes, sir."

"Hit it!"

Luis didn't need to be told twice. He was out of the dormitory with enviable swiftness and no trace of regret.

As he exited from Company C, however, he was accosted by a guard. This was a man who had a practice, deplored by all the inmates, of taking a paddle and giving a departing youth a few licks on the behind. The boys all saw that sort of thing as a "bad scene," but sometimes they could not avoid it.

"Where you going?" the man asked.

"I'm going home."

"Come here!" the guard called out with enthusiasm. "You're going to get your whipping!"

"I'll see you," Luis shot back.

"You better come here!"

"I'll see you. I'm gone!" Luis kept right on moving.

"When you come back," the guard promised irately, "you're going to get double!"

"*I ain't coming back!*" Luis exclaimed triumphantly. He headed straight for the administration building, his papers, and the bus.

At 9 o'clock Luis was happily seated on the vehicle that would transport him from the institution to the bus station in the city of Gatesville. As the buildings of the facility that had been his home for nearly four months receded into the distance, Luis scarcely bothered to look back. If he never saw them again, it would be far too soon.

The commercial bus out of Gatesville brought him into Waco, where the transfer to a Dallas bus was made with only minutes to spare. The last lap of the journey had now begun.

Luis's mind was filled with every enjoyable anticipation — home, family, friends, freedom! It seemed almost too good to be true that all this now awaited him after an absence much shorter than he had had any reason in the beginning to expect.

He did not at this moment recall the prayer he had prayed the night before his trip to Gatesville, when the loneliness and uncertainty had closed in around him. He did not pause just now to recollect how, while staring at the desolate construction site that loomed outside his window, he had asked his heavenly Father for help.

He did not remember this as his bus rolled on toward Dallas. But if he had, he would have known that his prayer had been answered.

9
No Cry for Help

But in a way he *did* remember.

"Have you ever heard of anyone being released from here after three months?" he had asked his fellow inmates at Company C. They agreed they had never heard of such a thing. Neither had Luis. So it was plain to him that a divine Hand had intervened on his behalf. Otherwise he would not be heading back to Dallas as he was right now.

Luis was conscious of this fact as he watched the fields and towns pass by outside the windows of his bus. But at the moment he was not inclined to think very deeply about it. Perhaps, in the excitement of going home, that was too much to expect him to do.

Even less was Luis inclined to consider that Gatesville had been more than a correctional facility for him. In fact it had also been a school. His Father in heaven had been the Teacher. And through the manifold problems and dangers that Gatesville had posed, the divine Instructor had been saying one thing above all else: "You need My help." Much depended on whether that lesson had been learned.

When the bus finally pulled in at the downtown terminal in Dallas, Luis's heart leaped to his throat. There, waiting to meet him, were his mother and his sisters, Mary and Christine. The embraces that followed were filled with genuine warmth and love. It was a welcome that Luis never forgot.

"Son, it's good to have you home," Julia told him.

"It's good to be back, Mother," he replied. Words could not express how good it really was.

The Rodriguez family now lived in a house that Luis had not seen before. It was located on Ferris Street almost directly behind the storefront church, which faced on Hickory Street. But strange house or not, the moment Luis walked through the door it was home. The sentiments which its atmosphere aroused in him were remembered for a long time afterward.

It was now early afternoon. There was plenty of time left in the day to look up some old friends. After a while Luis was out on the streets doing just that.

Mario Mendez lived only a few blocks from Luis. It had been Mario's friendship with the youth in the Gatesville butcher shop that had helped Luis to avoid a fight and a potential knifing. Mario greeted the returnee with the "wised up" lingo of the correctional facility. Luis shot back at him with the same thing.

"Come on, man!" Mario laughed. "You don't need that kind of talk anymore! You're back in the free world now!"

Luis joined in the laughter and the two of them sat down to reminisce and trade the latest news. Luis brought Mario up to date on the scene at Gatesville, while Mario described the happenings in the "Poso" and at City Park.

When evening came, Luis found himself at City Park. Such tensions as there had once been between "City" and "El Poso" had subsided now. A large number of boys from both areas had done time at Gatesville and had experienced the solidarity which that institution thrust upon them. City Park had become the favorite gathering spot for Latino youths from both sections of South Dallas. It was the ideal place for Luis to renew old acquaintances.

It was also a popular watering hole. Drinking was not allowed in the clubhouse, but if one prowled around the bushes and trees which dotted the park's extensive area, little knots of boys could be found enjoying liquid refreshments.

Inevitably Luis wandered into a group that was passing around a bottle of Thunderbird wine.

Before going to Gatesville, Luis had developed a strong preference for wine in general and for Thunderbird in particular. Though beer and wine could not legally be sold to minors, they were nevertheless readily available. Besides merchants who tended not to be too curious about the age of their customers, there were many individual entrepreneurs who serviced the needs of underaged drinkers. One of these was a well known figure in the "Poso," a black man who bore the suggestive nickname "Walking Dead." He had furnished many a bottle of spirits to his youthful customers, one of whom had been Luis.

It had been nearly four months since Luis had tasted any alcoholic beverage. As the Thunderbird passed from mouth to mouth, the memory of its exhilaration flashed across his mind.

What he did not recall was the dangerous excess which had begun to mark his use of wine in pre-Gatesville days. Thunderbird was clearly another old acquaintance which Luis felt he wanted to renew. He took his turn with the bottle.

But he made a surprising discovery. He didn't like it anymore! It didn't taste good! Gatesville had apparently robbed him of his taste for wine!

That was a benefit he did not particularly appreciate at this moment. He decided he would have to get some beer instead. Before the evening was over, he had celebrated his freedom with a can or two of a popular brew.

Luis slept soundly that night in his own bed. No cage door clanged shut as he retired. No keys jangled in any lock. It was his first night of freedom.

Or was it? Perhaps it was only his first night in another kind of cage.

In the days that followed, Luis rapidly acclimated himself again to life in the barrio. But there was a difference. He went back to church. That was something he had made up his mind to do while he was still at Gatesville. And now that he was home, he was strongly conscious of his obligation to God. Returning to church was the very least repayment he could make for the gracious help he had received in a place he hoped never to see again. It was not an unworthy motivation. It was simply an inadequate one.

Not long after his return to Dallas, Luis was coming out of a movie theater one Sunday afternoon. He had crossed Ervay Street and was making his way down a partially paved road in the general direction of church. He had about an hour-and-a-half before the meeting was to begin. A slow, leisurely walk would eat up some of that time, and the rest he could kill with judicious stops along the way.

Suddenly a car careened around the corner directly ahead of him. As it passed a female voice called his name. A few yards behind him, the car screeched to a stop and a young girl got out. She was obviously "loaded" on either liquor or dope.

"Hey, Luis! It's me! Mary Lou!" She was an Anglo girl.

"Hi, Mary Lou," Luis called back, assessing her condition as far gone.

"Come go with us, Luis," she suggested. Another girl and one boy were in the car.

"No, I can't. I'm going to church," Luis replied.

"Aw, c'mon and go with us!" Mary Lou persisted. "We're planning to party."

"I've gotta go to church."

"Okay, then, I'll go with you," Mary Lou decided.

"You can't go with me, Mary Lou!" Luis objected. *Not in that condition you can't!* he was thinking.

Mary Lou was not about to take no for an answer. Turning back to the occupants of the car, she instructed them to proceed without her. The car promptly pulled off. Luis was now stuck with Mary Lou.

But the couple had gone only a few steps when another car pulled up. This one was full of Latino boys, four or five of them, all of whom Luis knew.

"Hey, what's going on, Luis?" they called out through the vehicle's open windows. "Who's your girlfriend?"

"This is Mary Lou," Luis informed them.

"Why don't you two get in and come with us?" They had noted the girl's condition and it gave them ideas.

"I can't," Luis declined, "I'm going to church."

"Well, maybe Mary Lou wants to come," they suggested hopefully. "Mary Lou, you want to take a ride?"

"No, not if Luis don't come," Mary Lou replied.

"Aw, c'mon," they cajoled. "You sure look sweet today. We'll show you some fun."

"I'm not getting in that car if Luis don't get in," she insisted.

"C'mon, Luis," they renewed their entreaties, "she's not gonna get in if you don't."

"I told you," Luis repeated, "I gotta go to church."

"That's okay. We'll take you over there. Get in."

It seemed like a promising way to ditch Mary Lou. The two of them got into the car.

The boys soon learned that Luis did not have to be in church right away. Before he could raise much of a protest, they were headed for West Dallas. In Spanish, they discussed going to a secluded spot in the Trinity River bottoms, where they planned to have intercourse with their female rider.

Luis wanted no part of that. This was wrong. And he knew that if the girl were an unwilling participant, there could be trouble. He really *did* want to get to church that night, but he was beginning to wonder whether he would.

When they arrived in West Dallas, they drove to the location they had in mind, but it was still too light for any activity. Pulling out of the Trinity bottoms, they returned to Singleton Boulevard, intending to cruise for a while until darkness began to set in.

They had not gone very far before they attracted the attention of a police car. Its flashing signal beam warned them to stop.

Anxiety stirred in Luis over this unwanted development and intensified steadily as the situation deteriorated. The officers saw the condition of Mary Lou and suspected she had overdosed on drugs. Soon two other patrol cars had been summoned, along with an ambulance. The youths were dispersed into the cars under arrest, and the girl was rushed for treatment to Parkland Hospital. A substantial crowd of the curious had gathered by the time all the vehicles drove off.

Luis and his companions were now headed for jail. Among the four or five preliminary charges on which they were being detained, the most serious included investigation of narcotics, aggravated assault, and attempted rape. For any of these, a penitentiary sentence was a possible outcome. With Gatesville so recently behind him, Luis hardly dared even to think of such a result.

The building into which they were ushered by their police escort was later to gain national notoriety. It was the city jail at Harwood and Commerce Streets in downtown Dallas, where Jack Ruby would gun down Lee Harvey Oswald in the aftermath of the Kennedy assassination. But at the moment its only significance for Luis was its chilling threat of another imprisonment.

The boys were conducted to an office for interrogation. But by the time this process was in motion, word arrived from Parkland Hospital that the girl had cleared all of her male companions. She had also admitted being a runaway from Gainesville, the detention facility for girls which was the counterpart of the Gatesville school for boys. Mary Lou had done at least one good deed that day!

The most serious charges were promptly dropped. But the youths were informed that as minors they would be booked for violation of state liquor laws, since a bottle of whiskey had been found in their car. A night in jail and an undesirable blemish on his personal record were now in prospect for Luis.

Since this kind of trouble was also a violation of his Gatesville parole, potential complications lay ahead.

As the boys were led to the booking area, Luis turned to speak to the officer in charge of them.

"Officer, I haven't been drinking," he began. "I haven't had nothing to drink and I didn't have nothing with me."

"What were you doing with these guys, then?" the man wanted to know.

"I was just riding around with them, sir. But I haven't drunk nothing. I was on my way to church."

"You were on your way to church?" the officer's voice was edged with skepticism. "Why didn't you go ahead and go? Why did you go with them?"

"I don't know, sir."

"You were on your way to church, huh?"

"Yes, sir."

"You see that door over there?" the officer indicated the exit on the Harwood Street side. "Let's see how fast you can get through it."

"Yes, *sir!*"

As he broke away from the group, one of the other boys called after him.

"Tell Irma we're through," he requested. Apparently this trouble embarrassed him and he preferred not to face his girlfriend and try to explain it.

"Okay," Luis agreed. The next moment he was out of their sight.

The walk back to South Dallas was several miles long, but Luis was used to it. The whole sequence of events had actually transpired in a comparatively short time. If he hurried, he could still make it to church.

The handmade wooden benches had followed the church from its original clapboard home to the washateria building and then on to its present storefront location. Luis sat on one of them and listened to the sermon which was being preached. He could not help feeling that his presence here on this night was remarkable.

Indeed it was. But it was more than that. It was another demonstration that his heavenly Father knew the doorways out of trouble.

There was a striking similarity between the exit he had just made from the police station and his final departure from Gatesville. At the correctional facility it had been Mr. Smith who said, "Hit that door, Luis!" Downtown it had been the officer saying, "Let's see how fast you can get out that door!" But in both situations it had been his Father who had opened the door!

That was worth thinking about. The incident involving Mary Lou vibrated powerfully with the resonances of a crucial communication. It was as if the message of Gatesville was being replayed one more time. And its content was unchanged: "You need My help."

It was easier to hear that message within the confines of a juvenile prison. Out here it was much harder, and Luis failed to hear it. True enough, he had gone through an unusual experience just now. But from his own youthful perspective that was simply the way things "fell out."

Thus Luis had begun to face life differently in the "free world" than he had faced it while in confinement. Unlike the night before his trip to Gatesville, there was now no cry for help.

Later on, Luis told Irma that she and her boyfriend were through.

10
I'll Stop in a Minute

A screwdriver was their only implement. Its grinding, crunching sound seemed louder than it really was. But the hole in the door was now almost big enough to stick a hand through. Soon one of the boys reached inside and removed the heavy two-by-four which braced the entrance shut.

Mario, Cirilo, and Luis entered the deserted beer joint. Its interior was hardly familiar to them. They were not old enough to be at a place like this during business hours.

A raid on the establishment's jukebox, using the screwdriver to pry it open, yielded only some small change. But no matter. There was plenty of food and liquor around. They collected about a dozen bottles of champagne, several cases of beer, and a substantial amount of lunchmeat and bread. Then they went out by the rear entrance, through which they had come in.

As the youthful burglars made their way around the side of the building toward Akard Street, they received a sudden shock. Two figures were standing on the sidewalk immediately in front of them. A surge of fear that they were about to be caught swept over them. The fear subsided quickly, however, when the figures turned out to be a black man and his female companion.

Maybe it was relief, or a touch of generosity, or merely an effort to bribe these witnesses, but the boys offered the man a bottle of champagne. The gift was accepted, and he and his companion went on their way. So did Mario, Cirilo, and Luis.

Hugging the darkest streets and alleys, the companions transported their loot to a strange destination. This was an old automobile permanently parked in a garage on Hickory Street. It served as the current home of a boy named Alberto. Alberto was only too glad to welcome these guests and the goods they brought with them.

The four boys had a great deal in common. All of them were graduates of Gatesville. Cirilo was in fact the same youth who had wounded Miguel at the correctional facility and had precipitated Luis's hardest days at that institution.

Alberto, however, was not from Dallas. He had come to the city after his release from Gatesville even though he had no family here. The junk car furnished him with a place to spend his nights. An old hair dryer plugged into a socket in the garage supplied him with a meager amount of heat. This was a time of year when the nights tended to be uncomfortably cool.

The vehicle soon became the scene for a party. There was no way the four boys could consume all their stocks, but they made a valiant effort to do so. Using some champagne glasses which they had also removed from the bar, they began a round of toasts. In language as ribald as they could recollect or invent, they toasted every imaginable thing and swigged down champagne in impressive amounts. Thus warmed on the inside, they passed the hair dryer from hand to hand to gain some external comfort. Before long they all got exceedingly drunk.

At one point in this intoxicating celebration, Luis got out of the car to pry off the cap of a "longneck" bottle of beer. For this purpose he was trying to use a large nail that curved down from its spot in the wall of the garage. But his hand was so unsteady that he could barely make contact between the nail and the bottle.

"Look at that fool!" laughed one of his companions. "He can't even open a bottle of beer!"

So someone else did it for him.

It might have seemed strange that even when Luis was surrounded by former residents of the juvenile prison, the impact of his experiences there continued to fade. And yet it wasn't strange at all. The months were slipping by and Luis simply suffered from a malady that afflicts the hearts of people in all walks of life. In times of pressure and distress, it is easy to think about God. In better times, it is even easier not to.

At Gatesville, survival and freedom had been daily goals that weighed constantly on Luis's mind. But here in the barrio there were other things, such as acceptance with one's peers. If Luis had belonged to a more cultured level of society, he might have sought approval in more cultured ways. But in South Dallas, a youth found acceptance in behavior which the larger environment pronounced illegal.

Luis did not mind being called a fool in the joking way in which all the boys called each other that. But if he had rejected the lifestyle of his everyday companions, they would have called him something else. They would have called him a *puto*. The word suggested sexual deviance and constituted a stinging put-down. At 17, Luis was not prepared for that kind of rejection.

On his eighteenth birthday there was a party at Luis's home. Luis's father would not permit those in attendance to bring beer or wine into the house. But outside in the yard, or around the cars parked in the street, there was plenty to be had. Like many another similar Latino celebration, people milled in and about the residence in large numbers. Since the gathering was in Luis's honor, quite a few of these were teenagers or young men.

As anyone could have anticipated, the drinking led to an arousing of tempers. But before real trouble could start, someone made what seemed to be an inspired suggestion.

"Hey, if you want to fight," they proposed, "let's go to North Dallas."

It was an idea whose time had come. Soon about a dozen boys had piled into two cars and were headed toward "enemy territory." Naturally Luis was among them, savoring the excitement.

The hub of the North Dallas barrio was Pike's Park, situated on Harry Hines Boulevard just north of downtown. Next to the park and stretching some distance beyond it was a large public housing project which contained chiefly Hispanic inhabitants. It was to this area that the two vehicles made their way.

One automobile was driven by Fernando Cantrel, of "Dirty Dozen" fame. Cirilo was driving the car in which Luis was riding. As they approached the parking area which divided Pike's Park from the projects, they sighted a car containing two youths who were driving out.

"Block them, man," someone urged, but the car got by Cirilo's vehicle and headed up Harry Hines.

"Man, you let them out," the riders complained. "We could've put a beating on them."

"Say, man," Cirilo rejoined, "I couldn't let them hit this car. It belongs to my brother."

A short distance ahead, the other car with its two occupants turned into the projects. The South Dallas autos followed them in. By the time they had overtaken it, the vehicle they were pursuing was empty.

Determined to locate their victims, all but the two drivers piled out and divided up for the search. Making their way between the long, two-story apartment structures, they tracked their quarry without success. The route taken by the group which Luis was with led them to the rear of the project area along the grassy edge of a downhill slope.

All at once Luis looked around him and was startled to discover that he was alone on the slope. Suddenly there was the report of a .22 rifle as it fired a couple of shots. Glancing up at a nearby downstairs porch, he caught sight of the weapon in the hands of the boy who was using it.

"Luis, get down here," someone called. "They've got a gun."

Luis had always fancied himself a swift runner. The speed with which he got down the hill did nothing to disprove this. So fast was he moving, in fact, that he actually ran past the youths at the base of the slope and collided violently with a barbed-wire fence a few yards further on. The impact of the collision hurled him backward.

But he recovered swiftly and rejoined his companions.

"Let's get back up there," someone suggested. "The car is waiting for us in the parking lot."

"No, man!" another advised. "That dude may still be up there waiting on us with his gun!"

"What're we going to do?" wondered a less resolute voice.

"Let's go down the tracks," one youth advised. Some railroad tracks lay about 20 or 30 yards beyond the barbed-wire fence. "We can get into town that way and walk back to 'City.' "

"But they're waiting for us in the car," came the objection.

"They won't wait long," someone guessed. "They'll take out of there pretty soon if we don't come back. They'll get away."

"Okay, let's make it down the tracks."

The boys now ducked under or through the barbed wire and headed for the train tracks. Somewhere along this route, Luis observed that his T-shirt was bloody. When he removed it, he found an ugly, bleeding gash across his chest which was the result of his collision with the fence.

Without much success, he tried to wipe off the blood from his shirt. He didn't want to attract curiosity when they passed through the downtown area, especially not from the police.

Downtown the youths split up into pairs and took different routes back to South Dallas. This expedient reduced the possibility of police scrutiny. Everyone in the original party, including the drivers of the two cars, returned to their home turf unscathed. All, that is, except Luis, whose wound healed poorly and left him with an unattractive scar.

The fact that he could have come out of this escapade with much worse than a scar aroused in Luis a vague disquiet. Despite his growing conformity to the way of life around him, he could never erase from his consciousness a sort of nebulous feeling of guilt.

If he sat down with a beer, for example, something inside of him seemed to be saying, *It don't seem right. It's not the thing to be doing. What's happening?*

But this inner voice was not very loud. Church attendance had also become quite infrequent. His post-Gatesville determination to go back there and learn more had virtually

disappeared. The sense of urgent personal need which had
flowered so briefly in the hothouse environment of reform
school had withered under the wintry blasts of everyday life.

And Luis was getting away with the things he did. The
wound from the barbed-wire fence was the worst damage he
had suffered since his return to Dallas. The wise man of old
had been right when he said, "Because sentence against an evil
work is not executed speedily, therefore the hearts of the sons
of men is fully set in them to do evil."

Luis's steady slide into dissolute ways continued without
abatement.

Luis's family had now moved onto Hickory Street. Just up
the block, near Ervay, was the home of Chelo Peredes. Chelo
was the boy who had claimed Luis's wallet while Luis was still
a "freshfish" at Gatesville. But the incident was so far in the
past that if it were mentioned at all it would merely provoke
amusement and laughter. There was no reason why Luis
should not go to a party at Chelo's house, especially when it
was so near his own.

When he got there, Luis sat down on a swing on the front
porch. About a dozen boys were sitting or standing around on
the porch, most of them drinking. But someone had brought a
joint of marijuana. In those days, possession of even a single
joint was a daring and dangerous act. If caught, one could go to
prison.

The marijuana was passed to Luis.

"Light it up, Luis," his benefactor invited him.

"Gimme a match," Luis asked, accepting the joint.

But Luis had never used marijuana before and did not know
the proper way to "kick it open." When this became apparent,
the first youth took it back and demonstrated.

"Okay, I see," Luis responded. "Give it here."

Luis lighted the joint and drew on it like it was a regular
cigarette.

"Don't do it like that," someone advised.

"Why not?"

"You got to hold the smoke in."

"You'll choke on it," Luis objected.

"No, you won't. That's what gets you high." By this time the joint had passed to another boy.

"All right," Luis replied, "give it here. Let me try again."

"Don't give him no more," one youth interposed. "He don't know how to do it."

"No, I want to learn," Luis insisted. "Give it back."

And learn he did. In a few moments his world had become a movie in slow motion, and the swing on which he sat began to travel its arc with incredible listlessness.

"Look at old Luis!" he heard someone's voice saying. "He's as crazy as you want to get!"

But marijuana was not the only route to "craziness." There were also pills, particularly the "reds" and "yellowjackets" which were readily available at the inexpensive rate of three for 50 cents. Luis now added these to the undesirable practices he was accumulating.

Especially memorable was one party where his supplier was a youth named Julio Toscano. Julio was tall and skinny, with a high-pitched voice, a narrow face, and an abundance of bad habits. He looked the part of a small-time dealer.

Luis bought three "yellowjackets." After taking them, he came back to Julio.

"Hey, man," Luis told him, "those pills you sold me didn't do nothing. Give me three more."

Julio sold him these too. Luis took them and came back a third time.

"Julio, give me three more."

"Three more!" Julio exclaimed. "Man, I've already sold you six! What'd you do with *them*?"

"I lost those last three," Luis lied, "and the others didn't do nothing. I need three more."

Julio was pretty well spaced-out himself and was not inclined to probe things further. He parceled out the new supply.

Luis took them standing on some concrete steps in the frontyard of the house where the party was going on. It was Friday night and that was the last thing he remembered until Monday afternoon, when he woke up in bed at his own home. Who had brought him home he was never quite sure, and he never asked. His parents meanwhile maintained a complete silence about the incident.

But they were not always silent when Luis came home drunk or high on pills. On one such occasion he strolled into the kitchen to eat and ran into a buzz saw of parental displeasure. His father exploded first.

"Who do you think you are!" Luis Sr. stormed. "You're not even old enough to wipe your _____ and you're out there in the streets getting drunk or taking dope and getting somebody else to wipe your _____ for you! I don't want you around here anymore! You get out of this house and go live with those friends of yours! I'm not going to put up with this stuff anymore!"

Julia was also enraged. She communicated her estimate of Luis's lifestyle in language that was every bit as pungent as her husband's.

Luis was startled by this twin assault. It was not unusual for one or the other of them to communicate their opinions in emphatic terms, but the combination was awesome.

"I'm going to kill myself," Luis announced in tones he hoped sounded sufficiently wretched. Thereupon he got up and dashed upstairs to the bathroom, where there was a gas space heater. Once inside, he locked the door and turned on the gas.

By this time his parents had followed him upstairs and were banging on the bathroom door and shaking it. They were joined by Mary and Chris, who had rushed out of their room. After several minutes had passed, during which they all demanded that Luis unlock the door, they managed to get in.

Luis jumped to his feet. He had been lying on the floor with his face toward the entrance. An ample crack under the bathroom door served as a conduit for fresh air. Luis had been careful to breathe this while the heater discharged its gas!

The episode was not over. Luis retreated to his sisters' room. There he pulled out a pocket knife, which he had some difficulty in opening. When the weapon was finally focused on his chest, Luis observed that the family members, who had followed him to the room, did not move forward very rapidly to disarm him.

He then proceeded to pull up his T-shirt. The shirt would thereby be spared any damage when he struck the fatal blow! At last someone finally grabbed the knife.

"Foiled" again in his effort to make a dramatic exit from life, Luis went to his own room and closed the door. There he sat on the sill of an opened window waiting for his rescuers to arrive. When they did, he stuck one leg outside.

But that was as much as he was willing to venture. Luis was terrified of heights! He offered no resistance as he was pulled back in. Thereafter he decided to terminate his theatrics.

As was perfectly evident, Luis had no intention of killing himself. But his little performance had some of the traits of an unconscious psychodrama. The Bible warned that "he who pursues evil pursues it to his own death." Luis had no intention of pursuing evil that far, but he pursued it nevertheless. Someday a rescue might not arrive in time.

One night, after the clubhouse had closed, Luis and three of his friends were leaving City Park. They were proceeding via the walkway that led uphill to a street called Park Row. Suddenly they caught sight of a black youth dashing down the slope, hotly pursued by a detective.

"Stop or I'll shoot!" the detective shouted.

"I'll stop in a minute," the youth called back. But he kept right on going.

"Stop, I said!" repeated the officer.

"I'll stop in a minute," was the reply.

But the chase continued as the young black veered off to the far side of the clubhouse, circled it, and started back in the direction from which he had come.

"If you don't stop, I'll blow your head off," the detective warned.

"I'll stop in a minute," came the familiar refrain.

The four boys were the ones who actually stopped. The humor of the situation, coupled with its action, had caught their attention.

In a moment the lead runner shot past them only a few yards away. When the officer had reached the spot where the youthful observers were standing, he came to a halt himself.

He was obviously winded and happy for an excuse to abandon the chase. The fugitive quickly vanished from sight.

"What are you guys doing?" the detective asked.

"Nothing," they replied.

"What are you up to?" he persisted.

"Nothing!" they chorused sincerely.

"You got anything on you?"

"No, sir."

"Let's see."

The detective began to search them. He finally came up with a bullet which was in the pocket of one of Luis's companions.

"Where's the gun?" the officer wanted to know.

"We don't have one."

"Where were you going?"

"We were going home. The park just closed."

"I think you better come downtown. I'm taking you in for investigation."

Abruptly, one of the boys — Luis's old buddy Little Lupe — broke away from the group. He dashed down into a hollow that led past a swimming pool, then up again toward a street on the south side of the park.

"Hey, partner," the detective bellowed in what turned out to be a bluff, "there's one headed that way. Stop him!"

But nobody interfered with Little Lupe's escape. After a moment the other three boys were conducted to the partner's real location, a car parked to the east on Park Row. As he herded the youths into the vehicle, the detective addressed his companion.

"That nigger gave me the slip," he reported. "Did you see him?"

"No, I didn't," the other officer replied.

"Well, I found these guys down there. One of them had a bullet on him. I'm pulling them in for investigation."

It was the flimsiest of excuses. There was no law against carrying a bullet. It was the gun that mattered. The detective obviously wanted to save face, and Luis and his companions furnished him with a convenient way to do this.

A brief visit to the station at Harwood and Commerce Streets was followed by a prompt release. The walk back to South

Dallas was filled with lighthearted banter and good humor. All that the incident had really cost the boys was a detour on their way home. As compensation, they could laugh together about the chase at the park for weeks to come.

But Luis was running, too. He was running as hard as he could from that stable relationship with his heavenly Father on which his earthly future so fully depended. What he might have replied, if confronted with this fact, would have been hard to guess.

Maybe he would have said, "I'll stop in a minute."

11

At the Edge of the Precipice

Luis would have laughed if anyone had compared him with the flirtatious Mexican man of Hispanic tradition. *That* young man gave whistles and amorous glances to every woman in sight. He deserved the cold terror of the hideous skull he encountered one day.

Of course Luis was interested in girls, just as were all his Latino friends. He even intended to get married someday. Naturally he knew how to flirt as well as any of his companions did. He got plenty of practice.

But also like his companions, Luis chiefly flirted with trouble. It was a way of life in South Dallas, especially in one's late teenage years. And as in the tale he had heard long ago on the porch of his Floyd Street home, the outcome was foreordained. He would have to stare at the face of death.

Willie Richardson was a black teenager who hung out a great deal with the Latinos at City Park. That was not exactly the way it was supposed to be. The civil rights movement of the 1960's had not yet come, and public facilities in Dallas were still carefully segregated. But often the park supervisors pretended to be color-blind and overlooked his presence.

Willie had picked up a sprinkling of Spanish, mainly the *pachuco* talk used on the streets, and could carry on a limited conversation with his Hispanic friends. When allowed in the clubhouse for the dances on Thursday night, he proved to be a stylish partner for the Latino girls. His attendance at these events occasioned no surprise and, as a rule, no resentment.

One Thursday night, while one of these dances was in progress, Luis left the park clubhouse. He was heading in the direction of some benches where a group of youths was sipping beer. Hispanic boys usually believed that they danced their best only when they were a bit "loaded," and Luis was no exception. Soon he had taken a swallow or two from someone's quart of brew.

Suddenly a shot rang out from the direction of the swimming pool, which lay in the hollow just below the benches. This startled all the boys and they immediately imagined an enemy assault.

"It's North Dallas!" someone exclaimed. "They've come over to shoot it out!"

"Let's scatter!" another advised excitedly. "We don't know what they've got."

No one needed to be told a second time and the little knot of youths swiftly dispersed in several directions. But when there was no further gunfire and no sign of an advancing horde from the rival barrio, the boys began to peer down into the depression from which the sound had come.

"Hey," someone reported, "there's somebody lying down there. Looks like he's been shot."

"Who is it?"

"Don't know. Let's see."

Now a few braver souls made their way into the hollow where a prostrate form lay motionless, facedown.

"It's Willie," one of them called up the hill.

"How bad is he?" came the query.

"Looks bad, man!"

By the time Luis had come down, Willie's body had been turned over. It was clear that he had been shot in the middle of the forehead. There was blood on his face and on the ground.

"Is he dead?" someone inquired.

"I don't know. He's not moving."

"Somebody better get an ambulance."

"I'll go up to the clubhouse," Luis volunteered. "I'll get the man to call one."

Much shaken, Luis returned to the clubhouse. He was later to learn that his face was as white as a sheet when he reached the park supervisor.

"They shot Willie," he reported tensely.

"What? How bad is he?" the man wanted to know.

"I don't know. It looks bad. You better call an ambulance."

While this was being done, Luis returned to the hollow. The boys who crowded the area were now awed by something they thought they saw. On the ground where Willie's body had at first lain facedown, the blood stains seemed to resemble the shape of a cross.

"Hey look, Luis," one of them said, "Willie's blood is a cross!"

Luis looked. It was hard for him to be sure that he actually saw such a shape. Yet he knew what this meant to the others. Willie was with God.

"Who did this?" someone asked with a tone of anger. Willie was popular with the Latinos, who liked his easygoing ways.

"I don't know," came the reply.

"I heard he danced with Rosa," one youth reported. "I think Little Lupe was mad at him." Rosa was Little Lupe's girlfriend.

"Did Lupe do it?"

The ambulance had arrived and the attendants descended into the hollow, carrying a stretcher.

"That's a nigger!" one of them exclaimed. "We can't take *him!*" There was a special ambulance service for blacks.

"Hey, you *gotta* take him!" several youths insisted. "He's hurt bad!"

"He looks dead," came an attendant's callous reply. "We'll call for a nigger ambulance."

Willie's body remained unmoved until the other ambulance arrived. As the lifeless form was carried from the park, lively discussion continued among the Latino youths. Accumulating information suggested strongly that Little Lupe had indeed been the killer. Someone had even seen him with a .38 revolver.

"Lupe shouldn't have done that," one of them said. "Willie was all right."

"Yeah, man, he was okay."

"Let's get Lupe," another proposed.

"That's right! Let's get him!"

Determined on vengeance, the Latinos fanned out into the neighborhood in search of Little Lupe. Luis was with them. But Lupe had hidden somewhere, and their efforts to find him proved futile.

When Luis finally got home that night, his heart still boiled with rage. He angrily reported the killing to some of his family. Then, in a fit of fury, he took his pocket knife and hurled it across the room, where it lodged in the opposite wall.

The next day he returned to the scene of the shooting. He wanted to examine the bloodstains on the ground and to make up his mind whether or not they genuinely portrayed the outline of a cross. Examined in broad daylight, he could see why his friends had perceived such a shape. But he had to admit that the cross was not obvious at first glance.

Willie also had sometimes attended the storefront church, where Luis now only rarely appeared. Luis had heard that Willie had accepted the gift of divine life, as he himself had done so long ago. If that was true, then Willie really was with God whether there was a cross on the ground or not.

More than once Luis came back to the same spot. Finally the stains were worn away and the cross, if there had been one, was gone. But Luis knew in his heart that the only cross that mattered was the one on which Christ had died for his sins and Willie's. Luis liked to think that someday he would meet his easygoing black friend in heaven.

Meanwhile, Little Lupe had turned himself in and was sentenced to a term in Gatesville. It was light punishment for so serious a crime.

If the shooting of Willie Richardson had cast a shadow over Luis's experience, it was hardly surprising. The lifestyle that Luis had chosen invited such somber episodes. Although he did not realize it, more than at any period in his life thus far he had descended into the valley of the shadow of death.

One day, during this stretch of time, Luis was in the company of Mario Mendez. He and Mario were headed out of the very hollow in which Willie died and were walking toward Gano Street on the south side of the park. As they approached the street, a car with two men pulled to a stop. One of them was Mario's older brother, Pepe. The other was a man Luis had never seen before.

"Hey, Mario, come here," Pepe called out. Mario and Luis came up to the car.

"You want to buy a couple of joints?" Pepe inquired.

"Yeah, man. How much?" Mario wanted to know.

"Two bucks," Pepe replied.

"I don't have nothing on me, man. How about you, Luis?" Mario asked.

"Me neither. But maybe I can get a couple of bucks at home," Luis suggested.

"Okay, we'll wait for you," Mario and Pepe agreed.

Luis now crossed the street and started down a road which lay on one side of City Park School. He had only gone a short distance when the other man in the car got out and called after him.

"Say, man, wait a minute," the stranger requested.

"Yeah, what?" Luis called back.

"Are you Alfredo Gonzales?" the man asked.

"No," Luis replied.

"Do you know him?" the stranger continued.

"No, I don't."

"Are you sure?"

"Yeah, man, I'm sure. I don't know no Alfredo Gonzales," Luis assured him.

"Okay, then. That's cool."

The man turned to get back in the car and Luis continued on his way. It was not until several days later that Mario gave him some unsettling news.

"You know that dude that was with Pepe the other day?" Mario began.

"Yeah, what about him?" Luis asked.

"He was going to kill you, man. He thought you were Alfredo Gonzales. He got beat up one time by Alfredo and some other dudes. He had a pistol on him and he was going to shoot you."

It was a chilling thought. Luis had walked at the edge of the precipice without even knowing it. What if the man had not asked any questions? What if he had not believed the answers? Luis realized grimly that he himself might be in heaven right now.

But he shrugged it off. You couldn't let something like that bother you. That was the way life was, and this time things "fell out" okay.

Another time? Who could tell? And in South Dallas there was always another time.

One night there had been a big party on Ferris Street. A couple of girls were giving it, and the occasion attracted Latino boys like honey attracts bees. There were swarms of them — on the porch, in the yard, and around the house.

A lot of Luis's buddies were present, among them Mario, Cirilo, Cesario, and even Julio Toscano. But someone else was there whom Luis had never expected to see in this part of the city.

Placido!

Mario was particularly incensed at the presence of this notorious figure from the North Dallas barrio. He seethed with hostility, not only against Placido but against the two boys who had invited him. One of these was Carlos Peredes, an older brother of Chelo, and the other was Anselmo Salazar. Both were from South Dallas, so their hospitality seemed like an act of treachery.

It wasn't long before Luis found himself in a small group which included his old enemy from Gatesville. In the heated exchange of words that was taking place, he and Cirilo were backing up Mario, while Carlos, Anselmo, and two other youths were supporting Placido. They were standing on a cross street which intersected Ferris, on one side of the house where the party was going on.

"You better get the ____ out of here," Mario was telling Placido, "because if you don't we're sure as ____ going to whip your ____."

"Hey, man," Carlos interposed, "he's with us, man. If you jump on him, you'll have to jump on us, too."

"Cool it, Mario," Luis and Cirilo urged. "Be cool, man."

It had not gone unobserved by either of them that Carlos, Anselmo, and Placido, along with the two others, were armed. The outlines of their weapons, beneath their shirts at the waist, were unmistakably visible.

Mario was not easily calmed down.

"We don't want these punks coming over here into our territory," he fumed. "We got to send them back where they belong."

"Yeah, man, we know," Luis and Cirilo agreed as soothingly as possible, "but cool it for now. Let's go on into the party."

The three of them started to edge away.

"We're going to get it on, man," Mario shot back at Placido.

"If you jump him, you'll have to take us too," Carlos reminded him.

"Yeah, that's right!" Anselmo agreed.

The problem now was to find a weapon. If there was to be shooting, they wanted hardware. One possibility was a friend of theirs named Rogelio, who owned a .38 special. They walked over to him.

"Hey, Rogelio, go get your .38," they urged. "There's going to be trouble and we've got to have something."

"I loaned it to Mike's cousin," Rogelio responded. Mike's cousin was one of the boys in the group with Placido.

"See if you can get it from him, man."

"Okay, I'll try."

Rogelio now approached the youth in question.

"Look here, man," Rogelio told him, "I've gotta have that .38."

"I'll give it to you tomorrow," the boy replied.

"Not tomorrow, man. Now!" Rogelio insisted. "I need it now!"

"Hey, I can't right now, man. Like I said, I'll give it to you tomorrow."

The ploy had failed. The weapon stayed in the hands of a potential enemy. Meanwhile, Luis had gone inside the house to look for a youth who was nicknamed "Chulo." He knew that Chulo had a .22 automatic rifle back at his house, which was just up the block. When they came out together, Luis found Cirilo.

"Say, we're going up to Chulo's crib to get that .22 automatic," Luis informed him. "Don't start no problems while we're gone. Just be cool till we get back."

"Okay," Cirilo agreed, "but hurry, man!"

A swift trip to Chulo's house followed. Luis loaded the automatic with the maximum 18 shells. On the way back to the party, they heard gunfire. Luis and Chulo broke into a run.

Luis was carrying the automatic and was several steps ahead of Chulo. The house was situated on a corner just beyond the cross street, which Luis was rapidly approaching. But Luis was on the opposite side of Ferris Street from the house itself. As he got nearer, he quickly took in the main features of the situation.

Carlos, Anselmo, and Placido were on the sidewalk firing in the direction of the porch, where Mario was standing. So also were their two friends, including Mike's cousin, who now brandished the .38 he had refused to give up. All five were backing toward an automobile which belonged to Carlos and was parked on the cross street. Luis was therefore to their rear, across the intersection, and on the other side of Ferris Street. It was an ideal location.

Quickly Luis ducked behind a telephone pole. Without a moment's hesitation he began to unload his .22 in the direction of Placido and his allies. The shots startled the boys and they scrambled to conceal themselves behind their vehicle.

Then Luis made a mistake. He continued to fire until he had discharged all 18 shells. Now he had to pause and reload.

His opponents saw their chance. At once they aimed their pistols in his direction and loosed a fusillade of shots. Luis could hear some of these striking a house to his rear.

Luis decided it was time to retreat. He scurried back up Ferris Street toward Chulo's house. Chulo, who had never quite caught up with Luis, had the same idea and ran back ahead of him. Placido and his companions now piled into their cars and made good their escape.

Soon the streets blared with police sirens and were lit up with the flashing lights of squad cars. As quickly as the battle had erupted, it was over.

But Mario had been shot in the lower abdomen and had to be rushed to a hospital. It was a serious wound, but he managed to recover. Later it was learned that one of Luis's shots had struck Anselmo in the leg but did no permanent damage.

Both Carlos and Anselmo, however, had committed a cardinal sin. They had "jumped" for Placido and thus also for North Dallas. The same was true of Mike's cousin. They were now outcasts in their own part of town. For a long time they prudently avoided putting in an appearance at City Park or at any other scene where they might anticipate revenge.

Luis, on the other hand, had enhanced his standing with his peers. He had done what the code of the "jungle" demanded. He had come to the aid of a friend under attack.

In the days that followed, Luis did not bother to dwell on the personal danger to which this incident had exposed him. Though death had plainly cast its shadow across his path, he scarcely noticed. Instead, his mind was increasingly hardened to any kind of signal that the course he was following threatened him with complete disaster.

Luis certainly would have laughed to be told he resembled the flirtatious young man of Hispanic story. He would have been even more amused if informed that he was once again in prison.

But he was. As genuinely as he had been at Gatesville. The bars were invisible and the cage was bigger. Yet the prison was every bit as real.

Luis was trapped in the lifestyle of the barrio. Sin itself was his warden. He was fulfilling the words of the Lord Jesus Christ, who had warned, "Verily, verily I say to you, everyone who commits sin is the servant of sin."

Perhaps Luis should have recognized this prison. Here, too, he had encountered Placido!

12
Love Never Fails

No one was ever particularly surprised to hear a story about long-suffering parents who loyally stood by some wayward son or daughter. Parental love was the stuff of which such stories were made, and life was full of testimonies to the power of that kind of love.

It was strange that this sort of love was so rarely ascribed to God. If God's children behaved well, He acknowledged them. If they did not, they were surely not His children to begin with. Or even worse, He rejected them and cast them out of His family. These were the popular ideas about God's relationship to His sons and daughters. They were designed, of course, to protect His reputation. What they really did was to defame His fatherly love.

Fortunately these widespread notions were wrong. The divine promise still was, "I will never leave you nor forsake you." This guarantee remained true even when it was not believed. In fact the Bible also said, "If we are faithless, He remains faithful. He cannot deny Himself."

Something now happened in Luis's life which was an unmistakable token of his Father's fidelity. It came not in response to a cry for help from Luis, but as an unsolicited favor from a Heart infinitely filled with compassion. But as is so often the case, it was the kind of thing a casual observer might easily have overlooked.

In Gatesville, Luis had fallen in with some card-playing companions named Juanio, Huero, and Fred. Their friendship had helped him to stay out of trouble that he might otherwise have been tempted to get into. Now, in the moral "confinement" of the barrio, he found some new associates with whom he could while away his hours in much the same way. Their names were Sam, Cecilio, and Arnulfo.

Arnulfo, in fact, was one of the boys who had befriended the youth from the butcher shop at the correctional institution. He was once again to be an instrument for good in Luis's life.

Gradually Luis spent more and more time with these new companions. In a way there was nothing unusual about this. Among the Latinos, the smaller cliques of boys were only loose affiliations which could shift without discernible cause and without notice. Although Luis still saw Mario, Cirilo, and the others, he did not see them as often. This fact was very much to his advantage.

Sam, Cecil, and Arnulfo were not into stealing, as those other friends had been. Their main interests were poker, parties, beer, and girls, and not necessarily in that order. On the surface Luis's lifestyle remained unchanged. But without his being aware of it, the unseen hand of his Father had quietly reduced the growing level of physical danger to which he was being exposed. At the same time, the road was prepared for a profoundly important event in Luis's life.

Many of Luis's Latino acquaintances attended Crozier Technical High School. Although Luis and his closest companions had given up on school, they still took a lively interest in its social affairs. When a dance was held one night in the gym at Crozier Tech, Luis was there.

Luis had not spent many minutes mingling with the crowd of teenagers before he caught sight of Mona Esquivel. Mona was the oldest of three sisters who often put in an appearance at City Park, with the obvious intention of attracting the attention of the boys. A few times Luis had talked with Mona or taken a short walk with her. Mona had reached the unjustified conclusion that she and Luis were dating.

Luis knew what would happen if Mona saw him alone. She would latch onto him and everyone would think they were together. Since the Esquivel sisters were generally regarded as "easy," it would do nothing for Luis's reputation to be seen with her there. It was not a question of morality at all, but an issue of dignity. He knew the kind of ribbing he could expect from his friends if they thought he had taken Mona to the dance. Something had to be done to avoid this outcome.

Just then he noticed a girl named Felisita, who happened to be the sister of Mike Anguiano, whom Luis had met through his new circle of friends. Luis approached Feliz.

"Say, ain't you Mike's sister Feliz?" he began.

"Yes," she replied, "and you're Luis, aren't you? I've seen you with Mike."

"What's going on? What are you doing here?"

"Oh, I just came to dance."

"Well, I've been wanting to talk to you. You look real nice tonight. Would you like something to drink?" Luis asked.

"Yes, I think I'd like a Coke," Feliz replied.

"Okay, I'll get you one. I'll be right back."

Luis went out into a hallway that led off the gym and reached the concession stand.

"Two Cokes," he ordered. As luck would have it, Mona was standing close by.

"*Two* Cokes?" she repeated. "Who's the other one for?"

"Hi, Mona," Luis responded, "I didn't see you standing there."

"Who's the other Coke for?" Mona persisted.

"Oh, it's for a girl in there."

"You with a girl tonight?" Her voice now took on a note of wounded trust.

"I'm just talking to her, that's all," Luis explained, hoping he could make his retreat as quickly as possible.

"I thought we were going together," Mona returned with the steadily deepening overtones of one who has been betrayed.

"Mona, we're not going together," Luis replied emphatically. "We just talked a few times, that's all."

"But I thought we were."

"We're not, Mona. Listen, I gotta go now. See you around."

Without waiting for the inevitable protest, Luis picked up his Cokes and hurried back into the gym. To avoid any further encounters with Mona, he managed to spend the rest of the evening with Feliz. They sipped their Cokes together and danced a few records. And they talked that casual talk which fellows and girls have known how to talk since the beginning of time.

"Well, I guess I've got to go now," Feliz finally said. "I enjoyed talking to you."

"Me too," Luis replied. "See you around."

Feliz was an attractive girl with a beautiful olive complexion, delicate features, dark eyes, and a slender form. None of this had escaped Luis's notice, of course, but at the present time his first love was poker. He was currently working downtown for a company called Direct Delivery Service, so on paydays he had money for a stake. Poker had a lot more promise than trying to "beat the devil"!

One evening he was at Arnulfo's place absorbed in a game with several boys who happened to be there. Arnulfo came into the room.

"Hey, Luis! Feliz is outside," Arnulfo announced.

"Oh yeah? What's she doing?" Luis inquired casually, continuing to inspect his hand.

"She's in the car with Alicia. I picked them up at Alicia's house. Let's go riding," Arnulfo suggested. Alicia was a girl whom Arnulfo was seeing regularly.

"Hey, I can't go riding right now," Luis objected. "I'm in this game."

"Aw, c'mon," Arnulfo urged. "You know I can't go riding around with *two* girls in the car!"

"Not now, man. I'm getting ready to clean these guys out."

"Well, come on out for a minute anyway. I think she wants to talk to you."

After a bit more wheedling from Arnulfo, Luis finally consented to go outside. Through the car window he chatted briefly with Feliz.

"I'd like to go with you," he signed off, "but I'm in this poker game inside, so I guess I'll see you around. Be careful."

Arnulfo's matchmaking had failed for the moment. But he was not easily discouraged. A few times Luis was with him when he waited for Alicia to come out of Mass at the Catholic church on Harwood Street. The boys did not usually attend the service themselves, but they knew when the girls would get out. When Feliz appeared in the company of Alicia, naturally Luis wound up with her while Arnulfo squired Alicia. Then Arnulfo pulled a fast one.

It was early October in 1959 and the State Fair of Texas was in full swing at Fair Park. The final Friday of its two-week run was high-school day. Admitted on free passes, students swarmed over the fairgrounds and clogged the ever-popular Midway. If a teenager wanted to go to the fair at all, that was the day to do it.

"Luis! Let's go to the fair," Arnulfo proposed. "I've got my brother's car."

"I don't want to go to no fair," Luis countered. "What do I want to go down there for?"

"It's high-school night, man," Arnulfo reminded him. "There'll be lots of girls out there. We can meet some girls."

"I don't know, man. I'm looking for a poker game."

"Aw, c'mon. You can play poker any time. I want to see some girls!"

Finally giving in, Luis hopped into the car with his friend. Before long they were threading their way down the Midway through a mass of youthful humanity past the rides and concession stands and game booths, whose barkers shrilly competed with one another for business. It was truly the State Fair at its madcap best, and there were plenty of lovely lasses to ogle. Luis soon forgot all about poker.

About halfway down the concourse they reached a popular side area which featured a ride called the Himalaya. Above the din of a huge throng of milling teenage youths, the barker's microphone blared the repeated refrain, "You wanna go faaaster?" Invariably the riders responded with a ringing, "Yeeesss!" It was somewhere in here that the two friends sighted Alicia and Feliz. It was obvious that the encounter had been prearranged.

"Hey, man, you knew they were going to be here, didn't you?" Luis charged, managing to muster a mildly accusatory tone of voice.

"Yeah, I guess so," Arnulfo admitted. "But what the heck, we found some girls, didn't we?"

Luis couldn't deny that, and the rest of the evening he escorted Feliz around while Alicia accompanied Arnulfo. When the outing was over, Luis had no regrets. Feliz was fun to be with.

It wasn't long afterward, as the foursome was again together after a Sunday Mass, that Feliz asked an obvious question.

"Wouldn't you like to call me sometimes during the week?" she asked.

"Yeah, that'd be pretty good," Luis replied.

"Well, wouldn't you like to have my telephone number?" she continued.

"Yeah, I guess that would help," Luis agreed.

It did help, too. Nearly every weeknight thereafter Luis walked up to the pay phone at Ervay and Cigar Street and engaged Feliz in extended conversation. Since Feliz lived in the Oak Cliff section of Dallas and was rarely allowed out during the week, Luis made the most of these nightly communications by tying up the phone for a couple of hours at a time. Southwestern Bell soon took notice of this fact.

One night, when he had been on the phone quite a while, a car with two detectives pulled up to the curb. One of them got out and knocked on the door of the booth.

"Get off the phone," he called in, "I want to talk to you."

"Hey," Luis said, still speaking to Feliz, "the fuzz just pulled up."

"The police?"

"Yeah."

"What do they want?" Concern registered in her voice.

"I guess they want to talk to me."

"What about?"

"I don't know. They'll throw you in jail around here for no reason at all. I better let you go."

By this time the detective had lost patience and had pushed the door open. Luis hung up the phone.

"How long you been on the phone?" the man asked.

"Why?" Luis responded with a touch of impertinence in his tone.

"Because I asked you," the detective retorted.

"It ain't your dime," Luis shot back arrogantly.

"You want to keep your teeth?" the man inquired with a menacing glare.

"Yeah."

"Then you better start answering my questions. How long you been on that phone?"

"Oh, I don't know. Ten minutes maybe." It was a gross underestimation.

"You've been on for an hour-and-a-half!" the detective informed him. "They've been monitoring you down at the phone company. You've been overusing this phone every night of the week for a month."

"Well, I paid my money," Luis replied unsubdued. "I can use it as long as I want to."

"No, you can't. You can't tie it up like that. I want you to start getting off it a lot quicker, do you understand? We'll be running a check through here to see that you do."

With that warning, the detective got back in the car and the vehicle drove off.

Luis went home, but he was not to be so easily deterred. There was another pay phone down the street at the A & P, and he simply used that for a while. After a discreet period of days, he returned to the original booth and was never bothered again. Apparently the detectives had more weighty matters to concern them than to impede a budding teenage romance.

By late 1959, Luis and Feliz had agreed to go steady. Luis was driving a 1953 Plymouth convertible. When he was between jobs, he arranged to give Feliz transportation back and forth from school. This attracted the attention of *Tech Talk*, Crozier High's newsy newspaper.

"If you see a black and white convertible out back," it informed all its curious readers, "the fellow in it is taken — by Felisita Anguiano."

Once Luis jokingly bet Feliz she would not kiss him in front of the school. Feliz bet that she would. The test came one morning as he let her off.

"How about my kiss?" Luis asked.

"Uh uh," Feliz declined.

"We had a bet. Remember?"

"I'll give it to you tonight," she promised.

"I don't want it tonight. I want it now."

Feliz glanced at the crowd of students in front of Crozier Tech.

"Uh uh," she repeated. "Tonight." Then she slid out of the car.

Luis had won the bet while losing the kiss. More importantly, he was winning the girl. But it was not as though there was not an occasional setback.

Chelo Peredes now lived in Oak Cliff on the street directly behind the one where Feliz's family lived. One night Luis, Arnulfo, and Cecil were there drinking heavily. Cecil suggested that he and Luis go over to Feliz's house, and Luis readily agreed.

Feliz's mother was Cecil's aunt, so the visit seemed natural enough. But when Feliz saw Luis's intoxicated condition, she retreated to her bedroom and locked herself in. Eventually Luis passed out in one of the living-room chairs.

When he woke up the next morning, he was lying on a bed in Mike's room, to which someone had transported him. In the cold, sober light of dawn, he was deeply embarrassed.

"Let's get out of here," he urged his friend Cecil. "I don't want to be here when everybody wakes up." Least of all, when Feliz woke up!

But Feliz continued to see Luis. If beer had been a fatal disqualification for a husband, few Latino girls could have hoped for marriage. And marriage was a prospect that both of them entertained with increasing seriousness. One day, however, Luis told Feliz something which struck her as incredible.

They were driving together in the Plymouth and somehow the subject of religion came up.

"I know," Luis assured her with complete seriousness, "that if I was to die, I'd go to heaven."

"Luis," Feliz rejoined, "if you're going to heaven, everybody's going to heaven!"

It was natural for her to think that way, of course. Her remark merely reflected the popular opinion on this matter. You went to heaven if you deserved to. But Feliz did not realize that Jesus had said, "Verily, verily I say to you, he who believes on Me has eternal life." And eternal life was the very thing for which Luis had believed Him. Luis knew he could trust a promise from the Son of God.

It had not occurred to Luis, however, that God was about to give him another truly unmerited gift. For Luis was about to get a wife who was better than he deserved.

Yet on this subject also the Bible had spoken. "He who finds a wife finds a good thing, and obtains favor from the Lord."

13
A Roll of the Dice

It could hardly have been expected that Luis would look at the prospect of marriage as a favor from God. Even if he had, it was not certain how much he would have appreciated it.

Gratitude was not the hallmark of Luis's life. There was certainly a sense in which he valued God's gift of eternal life. But such appreciation as he felt for that gift was too shallow to have much effect on his behavior. The fact that his physical life had also been spared more than once was something he had virtually forgotten.

But God does not give His gifts only to those who receive them gratefully. Jesus had reminded His disciples that their Father in heaven "makes His sun to rise on the evil and on the good, and sends rain on the just and on the unjust." On another occasion He had said, "He is kind to the unthankful and to the evil."

Luis really did have a beneficent heavenly Father, who was about to be kind to him once again. But continuing ingratitude on Luis's part could easily lead to tragedy, and this time others would be involved besides himself.

It was now the spring of 1961. Luis's family had decided to go north to Indiana for several months to work in the tomato fields. All ten children in the Rodriguez household were old enough to help, including the three youngest girls, Rose Mary, Josephine, and Judy. Luis was going to go as well.

Or so he thought.

On the day of the family's departure, Luis assembled with his buddies to drink a few farewell rounds of beer. Their chosen rendezvous was a beer joint called Perry's on Forest Avenue. Arnulfo, Cecil, and Sam were all there to participate in this congenial sendoff. As the evening wore on toward 8 o'clock, Luis tore himself away.

"Hey, I gotta get back home," he announced. "I have to load up the car. They're probably waiting for me now."

When the final goodbyes were said, Luis hopped into his Plymouth and headed for the family residence, which was now in Oak Cliff. The family car was all but completely loaded when he arrived. His father greeted him with obvious annoyance.

"Where you been?" he asked impatiently.

"Just with the guys," Luis replied casually. "Just getting their address so I can write them a letter when I get up there."

"You been drinking?" his father inquired.

"Naw."

"You're drunk, aren't you?"

"No, I ain't drunk. I just had two or three beers with the guys, that's all."

"Well, you're not going to Indiana! I don't want you with us!"

"Why not?" Luis asked with some surprise.

"Because I don't want you going up there drunk, that's why!"

"I'll be sober by the time I get up there," was Luis's lighthearted reply. He couldn't really believe they intended to leave him behind. Anyway, he really *wasn't* drunk.

But Luis's father was adamant. Luis was not going to go and that's all there was to it. Luis was not about to beg for permission. After a while he got back into his Plymouth and drove off.

His destination, however, was just around the corner. There he kept vigil to see if his family really would depart without him, and to his amazement they did. It was hard for him to believe that this had happened, but there it was. He had not been separated from his family since Gatesville.

Luis decided to drive back to Perry's, where he found his friends still enjoying the farewell party without him. They were a bit startled to see him again. But they welcomed him to their circle anew and commiserated with him over some additional rounds of their favorite brew.

Eventually the group disbanded and went their separate ways. Luis decided to pass by Zane's apartment, which was not far away, and to report this turn of events. Then he headed for Oak Cliff.

The house on Maryland Street was shut up tight. Luis had to break in to gain access, but he was an old hand at that sort of thing. The problem came when he tried to sleep. It seemed to him that there were a million strange sounds in that house — creaky, cracky sounds —which came from every part of the large, two-story structure. Only the night before this very place had been a warm, inviting home, but tonight it could have been the tomb of Dracula!

Pretty soon Luis decided to sleep in the car.

It was not long after he dozed off that he heard someone rapping on the window of his Plymouth. A familiar voice was calling his name. It was Zane. Luis finished the night at Zane's place.

For the next six months, Luis lived at Zane's apartment. Ironically, this was situated in the barrio, which Luis and his family had moved out of when they took up residence in Oak Cliff. At night, whenever Luis came in early enough to do so, he and his preacher friend read the Bible together and prayed.

Luis had not done *that* much Bible reading since his days at Gatesville. But he found that he enjoyed it now, just as he had done then. Luis even took notes in his Bible so that he could remember the things he was learning.

The departure of his family found Luis without a job and without clothes. His clothing had all gone north in the family car. A search of the deserted house on Maryland Street turned up only a shirt and a pair of pants. That Friday, when he let Feliz off at her home, she handed him a package.

"Here," she said, "these are for you."

"What are they?" Luis asked.

"When you leave here, you can open them up," she replied and got out.

Luis did and discovered a much-needed commodity. Feliz had bought him some underwear! Leave it to Feliz to think about the basics of life!

Both of them were also thinking about marriage. Luis landed a job at a place called Circle T, helping to make corn dogs and TV dinners. When the family returned to Dallas at the end of summer, they were still miffed at Luis. They had expected him to follow them north to Indiana. "He'll be here any day now," they kept telling each other. But since he hadn't come, well, he could just go ahead and stay with Zane if that's what he wanted. Luis did, but that wasn't what he wanted. He wanted a home.

In December he and Feliz decided to tie the knot. Luis was now 20 years of age and Feliz was 18. Even if they had been older and more mature than they were, a happy and enduring marriage would have been difficult to achieve. In all segments of society, not just in the Latino culture, divorce rates were rising steeply. The odds against success in a youthful union like this were dishearteningly high.

Their families agreed with that assessment. On her side, Feliz had been solemnly warned against getting married to "a drunk." On Luis's side, the family was sure he was not yet ready to settle down. Both sets of parents washed their hands of the whole process and took no part in planning the nuptials. This foolish young couple were strictly on their own, they decided.

A Catholic wedding was out of the question. Luis was not Catholic and did not intend to raise his family in that particular faith. Though it might have seemed natural to ask Zane to perform the ceremony, Luis didn't bother. He knew this preacher did not want to unite in marriage a person who possessed eternal life with one who did not. But despite every impediment, the couple had made up their minds to go ahead.

Cecil was already married to a girl named Juanita. They offered their home as the site for the marriage and contacted a minister they knew to perform the service. Besides these hosts, the only other persons in attendance were Fernando Cantrel, once a moving spirit in the "Dirty Dozen," and his wife, Carmen. No members of either Luis's or Feliz's family chose to be there. The occasion did not provide that unalloyed rapture about which brides-to-be sometimes dream.

As everyone waited for the minister to arrive, Luis, Cecil, and Fernando improved the idle moments with a small-stakes game of dice. Once Feliz looked in on them.

"Luis," she remonstrated softly, "the preacher will be here any minute now. You all better quit your gambling."

"Yeah, I guess so," Luis agreed. Then he turned to his friends, "Let's quit till the man gets here. We can play after he leaves."

"Okay, that's cool," the others agreed.

The small-stakes game was terminated out of deference to the approaching ceremony. No one paused to reflect that the marriage itself was a high-stakes roll of the dice on which the happiness of several lives would depend.

The friends now sat around guzzling some beer. Before long, Feliz came in again.

"Luis," she pleaded, "you shouldn't be drinking tonight. We're getting married and you're going to be drunk."

"I'm not going to be drunk," Luis protested.

"Well, if you keep on drinking you are," she insisted.

"No, I won't."

"Well, just quit anyway. He'll be here in a minute."

Luis was still sober when the minister finally got there. In a quick and simple service he united the young couple in matrimony. Almost as soon as his duties were over, he left.

It was not long before the men resumed their dice game. Feliz, Juanita, and Carmen went downtown to see a movie called "A Pocketful of Miracles." If the marriage she had just entered into was going to work, Feliz would need a pocketful of these herself.

Husband and wife lived for a time with Cecil and Juanita in Oak Cliff. It was awkward trying to begin married life in someone else's house. They were both pleased when they found a little bungalow-type apartment around the corner on

Galloway. But their problems followed them to their new home.

Some of these were the kind you could laugh about later on. It was hard to forget the night Feliz cooked a batch of macaroni using a recipe Alicia had given her. The macaroni turned out to be something less than a gourmet's delight.

Luis had always been particular about his food, but on this night he made a valiant effort to eat. After a few minutes he looked up and saw that Feliz was crying.

"What's wrong, Fel?" he asked sympathetically.

"It's not cooked enough," Feliz replied in a teary voice. "It's no good."

"Oh, it's good," Luis said, stretching the truth a bit. "It just lacks a little, that's all."

"No, it's raw!" Feliz insisted, continuing to cry.

"Come on, Fel, don't cry. Let's sit over there." He got up and guided her to the sofa, where he put his arm around her and continued to console her.

After a while Feliz collected the offending macaroni and threw it down the commode. The result was a stopped-up toilet which required the attention of the landlord. He wondered what had caused the difficulty but the newlyweds professed ignorance. It was some time before Feliz tried that menu again!

But raw macaroni was the least of their marital concerns. Luis liked to come and go pretty much as he pleased. He was still employed at the corn dog place, while Feliz worked downtown at a finance company. The Plymouth was not in running condition, so both of them went back and forth to work on the bus. It was not uncommon for Feliz to return to an empty apartment and spend the rest of the evening by herself. Meanwhile Luis was out somewhere with his friends.

Feliz found this frightening. She was not used to being alone. She complained to her husband about his lack of consideration, but without much success.

One weekend she had to fend for herself while Luis took off with some friends from Circle T on a trip to the valley. She might never have seen her husband again had it not been for the unsolicited aid of the white Thunderbird and its mysterious driver.

That weekend excursion could have cost Luis his life. A later one cost him his job. Cirilo had joined the Army, but he continued to be one of Luis's most ill-omened companions. Unintentionally, he managed to complicate Luis's life once again.

One Sunday night Luis and Mario decided to drive Cirilo back to Fort Hood. On the return trip to Dallas, their vehicle broke down and Luis missed a day of work. When he appeared at Circle T the following morning, he was summarily fired.

This made a bad situation worse. Feliz was now the sole breadwinner in the new household. She continued to work while Luis drew unemployment compensation. As long as he was receiving this, his eagerness to find a job was less than intense. There were mornings that his wife thought he was out looking for work when he was actually back at the apartment asleep.

It was not a prescription for marital success.

But the supply of heaven-sent gifts had not yet been exhausted. Feliz was pregnant. She had not realized this at first and thought she had the flu. But her employer's wife recognized her symptoms and told her what her condition really was. A private physician was something the young couple could not afford. So Feliz now multiplied her use of the Dallas transit system as she traveled to and from the clinic at Baylor by bus.

When September arrived, the happy event was only weeks or days away. Early on the morning of the 23rd, her pains started. The Plymouth was back in running condition again and Luis excitedly helped her to the car. He made good time from their Oak Cliff home to Baylor Hospital, in East Dallas. As his wife lay in one of the small rooms in the maternity holding area, he held her hand and watched her suffer the agony of motherhood.

"Luis, Luis," she pleaded tearfully, "the pain is terrible. Tell the nurse to give me something."

"Okay, I'll talk to her," he replied gently, trying to sound calm. Then he went out to the nurses' station across the hall.

"Can you give my wife something?" he asked. "She's really hurting bad."

"We've already given her a shot," the nurse replied.

"Yes, but that's already worn off and she's hollering and screaming a lot. She needs something to help her."

"Those are her labor pains," the nurse responded in the accents of experience. "It's something she has to go through."

She was right, of course. There were some travails in life which could not be avoided. Luis went back into the room to hold Feliz's hand and to watch helplessly. Occasionally he had to step outside while a doctor and nurse attended his wife. Eventually he was banished altogether while Feliz was taken to delivery.

In a lounge area called "the dad's room," Luis sat down and waited nervously. He felt almost as powerless now as he had the night before his trip to Gatesville. So he did the same thing. He prayed.

"Father," he said in his heart, "Feliz is suffering a lot and I can't do nothing for her. Please help her."

This father to Father communication had joyful results. After a while Luis went back toward the nurses' station to get a progress report. As he entered that area, he saw a nurse coming up the hallway that led out of the delivery room. She was carrying a tiny bundle in her arms.

"Where's my boy?" Luis asked her.

"How did you know it was a boy?" she replied.

"I know it's a boy," Luis insisted confidently. "Just let me hold him."

The nurse placed the newborn infant in his father's arms. He was still covered with afterbirth and blood, but Luis was not looking at that. He was looking at his son. And dirty, messy little thing that he was, Luis loved him.

"We've got to wash him up," the nurse informed him, taking the baby back. "You can see him later at the viewing window. Your wife is going up to her room."

Luis watched the nurse go, touched for the first time with a father's joy. Little did he realize that this happiness was just an earthly reflection of the joy his heavenly Father had felt on that night years ago when Luis had become His son.

Spiritually, Luis was every bit as messy as his own boy had been a few moments before. But God had always been able to see His child through the unattractive afterbirth by which his life was disfigured. And He had been trying to wash that afterbirth away with the water of His Word. But it was sticky stuff and very resistant.

Luis Viviano Rodriguez saw the light of day at 8:16 A.M. that morning. His middle name was the legacy of his great grandfather, Viviano Canales. That was the valiant soul who had once routed a make-believe devil in a lonely Texas woods. Pretty soon, people on both sides of the family were calling the newborn infant Viviano more often than they called him Luis. In his great-grandson, this stout-hearted family forebear lived on.

But young Viviano would not be able to rout his own father's implacable Foe, who was an Adversary all too real. Despite the privilege and responsibility of parenthood, Luis continued to drift down a path which was winding its way toward catastrophe. Somewhere in the shadows ahead, his Enemy awaited him.

14
Bobby Is Dead

Hispanic traditions in the rearing of children were colorful and varied. If an infant experienced a sudden drop of any kind, the soft spot on the top of its head was believed to have sunk inward. This condition was described as *se le calló la moyera.*

The remedy was to place one's thumb in the child's mouth and press upward. Or the baby could be held by the feet head-down and a gentle tap administered to its tiny soles. This latter technique was Luis's favorite method with Viviano.

According to another popular belief, if someone saw an especially cute infant and failed to pick it up, the child would contract a fever. A sickness of this kind was referred to as *el ojo,* which meant "the eye." The *curado,* or cure, for *el ojo* was a distinctive one. An egg was broken into a cup or dish, and two strands of straw from a broom were laid across the yolk in the shape of a cross. The cup would be placed underneath the baby's crib at the point where its head lay. During the night the egg was believed to draw off the infant's fever.

Since it was normal for an egg to cook slowly at room temperature anyway, its appearance the next morning suggested that its task had been performed. If the baby was better, that was the final proof. But Luis regarded *el ojo* as pure superstition.

For a time after the birth of Viviano, Luis and Feliz lived with Luis's parents. On several occasions Julia Rodriquez employed this cure when her grandchild was ailing. One night Luis came in late and walked into his mother's room, where Viviano's bassinet was usually located. There he saw the egg and the cross-shaped straws underneath the bassinet.

"What's that thing under Viviano's crib?" Luis asked impatiently. He knew perfectly well what it was.

"You know what it is," his mother replied. "It's something you don't believe in, but it's going to do him some good."

"Get that thing out from under there!" Luis demanded with no attempt to conceal his disgust.

"He's sick, son," Julia remonstrated, *"Le hicieron ojo.* Someone saw him and didn't pick him up."

"He's just got a fever, that's all."

"Son, you just don't know about these things," his mother lectured him. "This is a *curado* that has worked many times."

"It ain't *never* worked!" Luis asserted flatly.

The exchange was faintly reminiscent of the occasion when Luis, as a little boy, had been told to "cut" an approaching storm with a butcher knife. That hadn't worked either.

"Why don't you just go to your room and let us take care of him," Julia suggested in a tone intended to communicate that the discussion was over.

"Take that stupid thing out from under him," Luis persisted undeterred.

"If you don't like the way we take care of your kid," his father chimed in, "why don't you just move out? We can look after him better than you can anyway. We raised ten of you, didn't we? Besides, you're always out getting drunk or something. You don't know nothing about being a father."

The atmosphere was now electric. Parents and son traded harsh words back and forth for several minutes. The invitation to move out was repeated once or twice more.

"Okay, I'll move out," Luis finally declared, "but I'm not leaving my boy here. My family's going with me."

Luis wasted no time keeping his promise. Even though it was now very late, he instructed Feliz to get ready to leave at once. After collecting a few belongings, they picked up Viviano and walked out into the night. The car was not working again, so they had to proceed on foot. It was also February, and the chill in the night air had even less healing potential for their son's fever than the *curado* they were leaving behind.

It was vintage Luis. He was wrong even when he was right. It was sensible to reject cultural superstitions like *el ojo*. But this headstrong lurch into the unknown was foolish. And the thoughtless manner in which he had dealt with everyone else on this night left much to be desired.

Small wonder he was such an inviting target for his Enemy. Caught up as he was in bad personal habits of long standing, trusting God only when he could think of nothing else to do, Luis might just as well have bared his chest for the decisive blow which his Adversary was eager to strike. If there was a hint of potential strength in his firm convictions, this was more than offset by the vulnerability which his impetuous nature bred. Luis clearly needed an emphatic warning about the dangers which he seemed to be courting. There was no need to take *el ojo* seriously. But Satan was another matter.

It was a long walk from Ewing Street, where Luis's parents lived, to the home of Feliz's family, on Pontiac. The couple was weary when they got there, but both they and Viviano survived the experience. Viviano, in fact, recovered as promptly from his fever as if the incident had never occurred. He never even missed the egg and the straws beneath his crib!

After a few days, Luis and Feliz rented a duplex apartment on La Salle Street, which was practically around the corner from Feliz's parents. Here the two of them settled down to the tasks of rearing a child and to a continuing assortment of tensions. The small, unimposing duplex home where they now lived was destined to be the scene of their severest trials.

Luis had been out of work again since shortly after Viviano's birth. But through the good offices of his wife's brother-in-law he was able to get a job on the sanitation crew at an A & P bakery. Cleaning lavatories and the like was certainly nothing to write home about. Still, the hours were good and on some days he got off as early as 1 o'clock. At first this new environment looked innocent enough, yet it was anything but that. In time it would prove to be a spiritual quagmire.

Luis was not long in getting on the wrong side of his employer. The manager at the bakery was eager to have all his workers give to a public fund-raising campaign called the United Way. In theory, contributions to this charitable undertaking were voluntary. But at the bakery, the pressure to give was direct and unblushing. Luis found this out one day when he went into the manager's office to pick up his check.

"Luis," his employer began, "next week's the deadline for giving to the United Way. Where's your pledge card?"

"It's in the trash," Luis informed him. "I ain't going to give nothing."

"Well, we want everybody to give," the man continued firmly. "We've always had 100 percent. We're very proud of that."

"I still ain't giving," Luis reiterated bluntly. "I need all my money myself."

The man glowered at him momentarily. "We expect everybody to give," he persisted. "Here's your pledge card."

Luis took the card and his check. He discarded the former and spent the latter. The next week the manager confronted him again.

"Where's your pledge card?" he wanted to know.

"It's in the trash."

"Well, if you don't give, you're not getting your check."

"You *have* to give me my check."

"Stand over there," the man instructed him, waving him out of the line of employees. After he had distributed the other checks, he returned his attention to Luis.

"Luis, you're going to have to give *something*. Everybody's giving."

"Well *I* ain't!"

"Then you're not getting your check."

"If you don't give me my check," Luis threatened, "I'm going to report you." At the moment he was not quite sure to whom.

"You've *got* to give something," the manager repeated, trying to make his demand sound as final as he could.

Luis reached into his pocket and pulled out a dime. Then he tossed it onto the manager's desk.

"Here, you can have *that!*" was his condescending retort.

The man's face blanched with indignation. "I'm going to fire you!" he shot back angrily.

"If you want to, go ahead," Luis replied. "Just give me my check."

The manager handed him his check and Luis left the office. But he was not fired. Luis had won the facedown, though he had scarcely enhanced his prospects at the A & P. In fact, he had begun to create a slippery situation for himself.

Still, he probably did need all of his money, since Feliz was pregnant again. By the time Luis was completing his first year at the A & P — and thereby setting a personal record for longevity on a job — the new arrival was imminent. In the wee hours of February 6, 1964, Luis became a father for the second time.

"I've got another boy," was the happy announcement with which he roused Zane by phone early that morning. Later he liked a suggestion his friend had made and called his newborn son Raul Ricardo Rodriguez. The child was too young to protest receiving his name from a "gringo" preacher!

The birth of a second son subtly enhanced Luis's feelings of manhood and self-esteem. Like most other Latino men, he experienced a special pride in possessing male offspring. At the bakery, this heightened sense of self-worth had an important manifestation.

The employees at the A & P had been partially organized by a weak local union. Since nearly a quarter of the workers had not joined it, the union had little bargaining power and was quietly tolerated by management. The sanitation crew especially suffered from this poor representation, working at wages well below those of other employees. Most of the cleanup people, in fact, were Hispanic.

The status quo was shattered, however, by the arrival in Dallas of an AFL-CIO organizer who targeted the bakery for special attention. His practiced eye soon detected in Luis the ideal go-between with the cleanup crew, who numbered from

15 to 20 strong. At a meeting attended by Luis and other key bakery employees, the organizer spoke glowingly of what a national union could accomplish for its members. He guaranteed to get the sanitation people an extra dollar-and-a-half an hour. That sounded pretty good to a two-time father like Luis.

Luis left the meeting with 50 dollars in union funds to be used to entertain his fellow workers and sell the virtues of the AFL-CIO. A few days later he assembled the cleanup men at the El Paso Cafe, across the railroad tracks from the bakery. After a couple rounds of beer, Luis made an announcement that was well received.

"Say, I've still got almost 25 dollars left," he reported.

"Spend it!" came the enthusiastic chorus.

Luis did so and fresh quarts of brew were served up all around until the funds were exhausted. In between quaffs Luis promoted his cause.

The organizer was eager to learn the measure of Luis's powers of persuasion.

"How many did you get to go along with us?" he asked hopefully.

"Everybody."

"Everybody?" The man's voice registered mild surprise.

"Yeah, everybody," Luis assured him. The organizer was impressed.

Luis's employer, however, was not. When the union handily won the election that followed, the manager of the bakery had yet another grudge to nurse against this hard-to-handle Latino janitor. In company with Miss Nichols of Stephen F. Austin School, the manager saw little in Luis beyond a rebellious personality.

But the union saw something else. It saw leadership. At a victory celebration in the organizer's apartment, Luis was pulled aside by a man from California. He too was Hispanic and had been brought in by the union for the last few days of the campaign at the bakery.

"Listen, man" he began in Spanish, "I've heard a lot of good things about you and I'm going to make you an offer. How would you like to work for the union and travel around and organize? I think you could do a real good job."

Luis was cool to this idea. "I don't know," he replied, "I'm not sure I want to do that. I've got a family here and I don't think I'd be interested."

"It's good money," the man pressed him. "You can make a thousand dollars a month plus expenses. And it's not all work, either. You'd be traveling and seeing new places and having a lot of fun, too."

It was an attractive offer. A thousand a month in the 60's was not exactly small change. The travel appealed to Luis as well.

"All right, maybe I'll think it over," he consented. "I'll have to talk to my wife, though. If I'm interested, I'll get back with you."

"Okay, that's fine," the man agreed. "I'll be here a few more days and I hope I hear from you. Give it some thought. It's a good deal."

When Luis brought the matter up at home, Feliz reacted as he had expected her to do. She didn't like the idea.

"You'll be away too much," she objected, "and the boys need you. You might be gone five or six weeks at a time, and that's too long. I don't want you to go."

Luis was inclined to agree with her. With Raul only a few months old, he was not excited by the idea of being away from his family for long stretches of time. A career as a union organizer had its attractions, but Luis decided to forgo it. For once a sense of parental responsibility had prevailed over the lure of a fast life. It was a good decision.

What snares Luis might have encountered in faraway cities he would now never know. Nevertheless, there were plenty of snares near at hand.

One morning Luis had to go into work at 5 o'clock. It was still dark when he pulled into the parking area at the bakery. No sooner had he killed his motor and cut off his lights than he noticed some peculiar activity.

Several men, all employees of the bakery, were scurrying back and forth between the building and the open trunks of several cars. It was obvious that they were placing something into the trunks.

Luis got out and called to a man named Martin, who was his supervisor.

"What are you doing, Martin?" he asked.

But by this time Luis thought he knew. The A & P warehouse adjoined the bakery and could be entered by climbing over a wire fence on the fourth floor. On the other three floors a wall sealed off the warehouse from the bakery area, but on that floor access was relatively easy. Luis knew that the cans the men were carrying had come from the warehouse.

"Open your trunk, Luis," was Martin's response.

"Why? What for?"

"Open your trunk. I got something for you."

"I don't want none of that."

"I got a couple cans of ham for you," Martin persisted. "Open up."

"I don't want none," Luis repeated.

"You'll open that trunk — or else!"

It was a perfect trap. The Enemy worked through Martin's lips and in Luis's mind all at the same time. Luis thought painfully of the shaky ground on which he stood with the manager, who bore him no love. Vividly he imagined Martin and his cohorts concocting a story which could get him fired. Maybe they would even blame this theft on him if he declined to become their partner in it. He had two kids to support, didn't he?

Luis opened his trunk.

There had been a time in the not too distant past when receiving stolen goods would not have bothered Luis at all. That it did so now had a strange explanation. It was one that spoke volumes about his vulnerability to his Adversary's enticements.

The explanation was rooted in the environment of the bakery. Since coming to the A & P, Luis had become an almost daily patron of the El Paso Cafe. Because he got off his job in the early afternoon and had plenty of time to kill before Feliz got off from hers, the café seemed like a natural place to consume his idle hours. He was now so much a part of the scenery there, that he often went into the kitchen to cook his own food. He had not lost the culinary skills he had acquired at Gatesville, and these enabled him to prepare his cuisine without onions.

But Luis's primary fare at the El Paso Cafe was beer. Starting on his first can so early in the day had a predictable result. By the time he ought to have gone for Feliz, he was frequently drunk. When that was true, he often did not go for her at all.

It was a distressing ordeal for Feliz to bear. When her husband failed to appear well after her 4:30 quitting time, she would have to call her brother or someone else to give her a ride. Alone in their La Salle Street home with two young children, she could never anticipate when Luis might put in his appearance, which all too commonly was late that night.

It was hard to decide which was worse, her husband's late arrival or the intoxicated state in which he arrived. In any case, on such days she had to put up with both.

Luis's father had admonished Feliz more than once about this kind of situation.

"Never go look for him," he had told her. "Ladies ought not to be in such places."

But she went one time, and the moment she stepped through the door of the café she was sorry she had. It seemed to her that the place was filled with drunken men. Her father-in-law had been right, and she never tried that again.

She did try to talk to Luis, however. But only when he was sober.

"Luis," she would remonstrate in her typically gentle way, "your drinking is hurting our marriage. It's coming between us as husband and wife and you're not being a father to your boys. You've got to quit it and start looking after your family the way you should."

Luis's buddies sometimes told him he was impossible to get along with when he was drunk. In such a condition he would have argued with Feliz. But sober he usually greeted her words with silence. What could he say? He knew she was right.

Slowly — much too slowly — the realization was dawning on Luis that God had not only favored him with two sons but with a wife who loved him. There was now an increasingly disquieting sense of guilt which had to be dealt with in some fashion. His way of dealing with it was indirect and ineffective.

Luis liked his beer too much to diminish his drinking. But to compensate for evading this problem, he decided to stop stealing! This permitted him to indulge the reassuring thought that his life was actually improving!

It was a form of self-deception which the incident in the bakery parking lot should have unmasked. Nothing less than a full submission to his heavenly Father could protect him from his Foe's devices. If this was not forthcoming, there could be fatal results. In fact, a warning of these was on its way.

Among all the Rodriguez brothers — five of them altogether — none was more popular with the whole family than John, whom everybody usually called "Bobby." It was a rare occasion when Bobby was not cheerful and friendly, and his happy-go-lucky disposition endeared him to the entire clan. Yet, strangely, Bobby also had some traits of a loner.

Along with most of the ten children of Luis and Julia Rodriguez, Bobby had once regularly attended the storefront church where his older brother had met God. Somewhere in those years Bobby too had accepted the same gift of divine life that Luis had received. But also like Luis, he had never learned to walk closely with his heavenly Father. In this respect as well, Bobby was a loner.

Bobby had married only a couple of months after Luis and Feliz. He too had two children, a boy and a girl. But unlike his elder sibling, he had not managed to hold his marriage together. He and his wife were separated, and Bobby was once again living with his parents in Oak Cliff. Nearly every day he took the long walk from the family residence to the old neighborhood in South Dallas. He was usually by himself when he did this, and what went through his mind on these lonesome treks no one ever knew.

Bobby loved Viviano and Raul. When he and his brother Robert visited Luis on La Salle, they happily played with their two young nephews. To the horror of Feliz, they liked to toss the boys to each other across the living room. They never failed to make the necessary catch, but a distraught mother was sure that someday they would!

A strange contradiction marked Bobby's life. Unlike the vast majority of young Hispanic men, Bobby didn't drink or smoke. That was a kind of residual influence from his years at church, which he never lost. But Bobby was a ladies' man who loved to attend dances and "make time" with the young girls. Much too substantially he seemed to incarnate the man in the Mexican legend whose addiction to dancing had led him into the company of the devil.

Odulia was one of the girls he had met at a dance. She was separated from her husband just as Bobby was from his wife. Perhaps this helped draw them together. But the affair into which they entered was not only wrong, but dangerous. It aroused the hostility of Odulia's estranged husband, who happened to be from North Dallas.

Since Bobby was a native of the rival barrio, the husband's natural animosity was sharply intensified. Vengefully, the young man made plans to catch Bobby at a dance and to eliminate him as a rival for his wife's affections.

Luis himself could have been caught up in that. An assault on Bobby would have invoked the code of retribution by which Luis had grown up. A fatal assault would have called for a comparable recompense. Bobby's behavior now endangered the happiness and welfare of many people.

It was on a Sunday in May of 1965 when Bobby decided to drive his friend Manuel to Oklahoma. Manuel was in the military service and was returning to his base after a week-end's leave. Odulia consented to make the trip with them.

On Monday morning on his way to work, Luis stopped by his parents' Oak Cliff residence to leave Viviano and Raul in the care of their grandmother. The argument over *el ojo* was now a thing of the past and the solidarity of the Rodriguez family had long since reasserted itself. But on this morning Luis found his mother obviously anxious.

"Bobby didn't come in last night," Julia informed him. "He told me he'd be in about 2 o'clock."

"Don't worry, Mother," Luis tried to reassure her, "he'll be in."

"But he should have been in a long time ago," Julia continued. "I'm worried something might have happened to him."

Julia loved all her children, but everyone knew her special feelings for Bobby. In the best traditions of Mexico he was considerate and extremely well-mannered toward elderly people. He treated his parents well and helped them in ways that the other children did not. He was easy to love.

"Please don't worry, Mother," Luis urged her again. "He'll probably be here before you know it. I'll see you tonight."

But as Luis drove away from the house, a powerful premonition took hold of him which he never forgot.

Bobby's dead! he said to himself. *He ain't never coming back! He ain't never going to walk in that house again!*

Luis used the 10 o'clock break to pick up breakfast at the El Paso Cafe. When he returned to the bakery, he was told that his parents had called. Unable to find him, they had left their message with his brother-in-law, Lapo, who worked at the warehouse.

"You'd better go talk to your brother-in-law," someone advised him. "He's got a message for you."

Luis headed for the elevator, which Lapo operated. When the elevator door opened, they were facing each other.

"Bobby's dead, isn't he?" Luis asked his startled in-law before the other could say anything himself.

Lapo appeared to be at a loss for words.

"Is that what you wanted to tell me?" Luis inquired again.

"You'd better call home," was Lapo's only response.

"Is Bobby dead or is one of the kids hurt?" Luis persisted.

"Yeah."

"Bobby's dead?"

"Yeah. You'd better call your mother."

Luis went to Martin and got permission to leave. There was chaos at home. Bobby had died in a car accident on his way back from Oklahoma. Odulia was also dead. Details were sketchy and the family wondered how to get the body home. A call to a funeral home settled this problem, but the emotional upheaval was slow to subside.

Bobby had always been a reckless driver, pushing a vehicle with the same intensity as he often pushed himself. Someone later observed, in a true piece of Hispanic wisdom, that his life had been so short because it had been so fast.

The car in which Bobby and Odulia were returning to Dallas had gone off the highway in the vicinity of Bowie, Texas. It had sped down into a ravine and up again, missing a couple of trees but crashing into a boulder. Bobby was thrown into the windshield and evidently died instantly of a broken neck. There was evidence that the girl had lived for several hours, crawling out the window perhaps to look for help, then crawling back into the car to die next to Bobby.

The ravine hid the wrecked vehicle from cars passing on the highway above it. The battery had been disabled so that there were no telltale lights or a blowing horn. It was only the next morning that a farmer plowing his field sighted the tragedy and summoned police.

When the body was returned to Dallas, in accordance with Hispanic custom it was brought in the casket to the family residence. There the departed loved one would spend a final night under the family roof. As at all such wakes, the home was filled with friends and relatives who came to pay their respects. Food was furnished lavishly by many of the callers, and the kitchen bulged with quantities of enchiladas, tamales, tortillas, Mexican breads, and other edibles.

The atmosphere of the gathering was restrained and subdued, but not baleful. Someone was always present in the living room, where the casket had been placed, for it was regarded as improper to leave the body alone. But visitors came and went, ate in the kitchen, chatted outside, and even slept in a bedroom if they decided to stay all night. In the presence of the deceased, soft and respectful conversation was carried on. About 8 o'clock a priest said Rosary. Nothing drew Hispanic people together more warmly or more movingly than an opportunity to comfort the bereaved. At such times the sense of community was powerful and reassuring.

On the day of the wake, Luis and his mother were standing in the living room. Julia commented on the appearance of the body.

"He looks just like himself, doesn't he?" she remarked. "There's even a smile on his face like he always had."

"Yes, he looks good," Luis agreed.

"We're going to miss him." Her voice quavered ever so slightly. "We loved him."

"Yeah. He brought a lot of happiness." Then Luis added, "But Bobby's in heaven now. He doesn't have any more pain."

Mrs. Rodriguez greeted this remark with respectful silence. Luis continued.

"Bobby believed. That's what it took."

No one knew better than Luis that it didn't take more than that. Luis himself had nothing more. Neither did Bobby. But both had responded with childlike simplicity to the divine offer: "Whoever wishes, let him take the water of life freely." It was not for nothing that Jesus had declared, "Whoever does not receive the kingdom of God as a little child will by no means enter into it."

That same day, Luis and Feliz were in the car together heading toward their La Salle Street house. Luis felt like talking to her about Bobby and about herself.

"Bobby's in heaven," he began.

Feliz offered no reply. She knew that Bobby had been going with another man's wife before he died, and that this had led to the girl's death as well as his own. Heaven did not seem like a probable destination in a case like this.

"Bobby was saved," Luis continued. "He had eternal life. You need to get saved too. All you have to do is believe."

The silence continued. It was all very confusing to Feliz. How could Luis be going to heaven with the kind of life he was living? She was better than he was, and did *she* need to get saved?

And yet she had to admit that she sometimes wondered if she did. On those widely scattered occasions when Luis took the family to the storefront church, it always seemed that the messages were directed at *her*. But why at her, when she had this sinner of a husband sitting next to her? *He* was the one who needed to be preached to!

What she did not know was that Luis's heavenly Father had His own ways of preaching to His disobedient son. Bobby's death was one of those ways. That's why Luis was preaching to Feliz right now.

But had Luis really understood his Father's communication? Its main point was clearly worth pondering. Sometimes God called his wayward children home.

15
Here Walks My Enemy

Luis did not pause to consider very long or very deeply the meaning of his brother's death. To him it was one of those inexplicable tragedies of life which God alone understood.

In a sense he was right. But at the same time he ought to have been warned by it. Luis knew that the Bible said, "Whom the Lord loves He corrects." He understood that the hand of his Father in heaven was often stretched out in discipline to His children. But he had not yet clearly realized that this discipline could actually terminate one's earthly life. That was in the Bible too, but Luis had forgotten about it. Perhaps, if he had taken time to think, he would have remembered.

Even so, such an awareness on Luis's part might not have altered the events which followed. He had been ignoring divine counsel for too long. For too long he had been roaming the trackless wasteland of moral and spiritual neglect. And that was dangerous territory to inhabit, for here walked his Enemy.

Luis himself, therefore, had created the conditions under which the Adversary could launch his most deadly assault. It was almost as if Luis was prodding him into action, just as years before he had prodded the dogs next door to the clapboard church. And this time his Foe drew from his arsenal a new weapon whose destructive potential was more appalling than any he had used before.

For an opening maneuver, the Enemy selected as his agent a young Hispanic from Corpus Christi. By what was anything but a coincidence, he found employment in Dallas at the A & P bakery, where he worked in production. Naturally he and Luis became acquainted.

Luis was now driving a brand-new Pontiac Le Mans. Thanks to the efforts of the union which he had served so well, Luis was currently making more money than he had on any previous job. His first new car was one obvious result of that. In the eyes of Feliz, a swelled head was another!

One day after work Luis stopped off according to his custom at the El Paso Cafe. José, the fellow from Corpus, was there that day and they began drinking together. With the Le Mans for transportation they decided to continue this activity at one or two other popular watering holes. Somewhere along this route they decided on a change of plans.

"Say, man," José spoke up, "you smoke marijuana?"

"You got any?" was Luis's reply.

"Yeah, man," José assured him, "I brought some up from Corpus. It ain't even been cleaned yet. It's still got the seeds and everything. We've got most of a plant."

"Where's it at?" Luis wanted to know.

"Back at my apartment."

"Let's go get it," Luis proposed.

"It's not clean, man."

"I know. You said that. We'll clean it."

"Okay, let's go then," José agreed. "I'm out at some courts on Fort Worth Avenue."

The Le Mans shot off in the direction of Fort Worth Avenue. When they reached their destination, Luis sat in the car while José went inside. Pretty soon he came out with a brown paper bag. Inside was part of a marijuana plant complete with leaves, seeds, and stalk. José got back in the car.

"Hey, my brother's inside," José informed him. "He just got up from Corpus."

"Is that so?" Luis responded casually. He could not have guessed that such a simple fact was part of the snare that had been laid for him.

The Le Mans was on its way again. While Luis drove, José labored to clean his Mary Jane and roll it into the cigarette paper used for this purpose. When enough joints had been prepared, they pulled off somewhere and began to smoke.

As the exhilarating fumes lifted his inward spirits, Luis complimented his benefactor. "This is good weed, man," he observed as if he were a user with long experience.

"Yeah. You can't beat it," José agreed.

Luis did not later recollect much else. He got home that evening without event, although he did recall waiting at a stop sign for a car that was still a good half-mile away. But under the influence of marijuana all objects moved as languidly as that car seemed to move. One could not take the chance that it was not actually bearing down more swiftly. Marijuana turned everything into a leisurely dream from which there was always the danger that you might awake with a resounding crash. But there was more than one way to crash.

On the next and the following day there was no sign of José at the bakery. This disturbed Luis considerably, since the bag containing the illegal weed had been left in his car. Though he had put it out of sight in the trunk, Luis was eager to return it to its owner. If for any reason he were stopped by the police and his car searched, he would be in big trouble. The raw state of the drug would be presumptive evidence that Luis was a dealer, and the penalties for that were stiff indeed. Ten years in the penitentiary would be a high price to pay for someone else's Mary Jane. Luis devoutly hoped it would never come to that.

He *had* to get rid of the marijuana!

After work Luis drove out to the courts on Fort Worth Avenue to return his unwanted cargo to José. But José wasn't there. On a second trip the manager had unsettling news for him.

"José? He's gone. He left for Corpus two days ago."

Then it dawned on Luis. His brother! His brother had come up to get him, and now José was gone for good. What was he going to do with the marijuana now?

For reasons that were largely inexplicable, he did not seriously consider simply throwing it away. Dangerous though possession of it was, the plant was a valuable commodity which Luis irrationally assumed deserved to get back into circulation. But at the same time he had no intention of selling it, although the amount he had — about a quarter of a pound — would have brought a good price.

Soon afterward he found himself in the company of a Latino named Gerardo. Gerardo had been around and seen a few things, so Luis shared his problem.

"Say, I've got this sack of marijuana in my car," he informed him. "I think there's about a quarter of a pound and I don't want to just throw it away, but I don't know what to do with it. I can't just carry it around with me. I might get busted."

"Yeah, that's right," Gerardo agreed, "but I think I know what you can do with it."

"It ain't been cleaned up yet," Luis advised him, "but I smoked some and it's good stuff."

"I know some people who'll take it," his friend observed knowingly.

"Yeah? Let's go give it to them." *The faster the better!* Luis was thinking.

In the Le Mans, Luis and Gerardo drove to a private residence. Gerardo went inside and returned after a short time with another man.

"What you got?" the man asked, bending his head down to the car window.

"About a quarter pound of pure weed," Luis replied.

"What do you want to do with it?"

"I was just going to throw it away."

"You don't need to do that. We can put it with our stuff," the dealer suggested.

"It's good weed," Luis declared, as if he were trying to make a sale. "It hasn't even been cut yet."

"Come on inside," was the friendly response.

The man led Luis and Gerardo inside the house and into a back bedroom. Luis was startled by what he saw. Six or seven men were seated on or near a large bed, rolling marijuana. The amount of marijuana spread out on the bed was more than Luis had ever seen in his life. There might have been as much as five pounds there. That this was a major operation was a self-evident and alarming fact.

Luis was eager to get away. He quickly turned over his own small cache to the operatives in the bedroom.

"Go ahead and get youselves some joints," offered their host genially.

"No, I got to go," Luis replied. But almost as soon as he said it, he knew he had made a mistake. To walk hastily in and out of a setup like this would arouse the gravest suspicions and expose him to potential danger.

Gerardo cast him a disapproving glance. "Why do you have to leave so fast?" he asked. "Let's stay awhile."

"Okay," Luis agreed, reversing his field, "I guess I don't have to be no place right away."

For the next hour-and-a-half, Luis nervously occupied a chair in the bedroom while the illicit activity continued. Even the couple of joints he lit up did not seem to ease his tensions very much. Suppose the police were to burst in on this thing? Luis would be caught right in the middle of a huge drug bust, and a term in the penitentiary would be a virtual certainty. The very thought was anguishing.

The relief he felt when Gerardo suggested they go was immense. It did not occur to him that he had walked right into his Enemy's trap. Still less did he consider why the trap had not been sprung. Getting away from the place was all that mattered, and he never went back. At least not to *that* place.

If Luis was intended to learn wisdom from so sobering an encounter with the Latino drug culture, that intention was not achieved. On the contrary, when the initial fear had passed, Luis was an even softer target for his Adversary's diverse techniques. A snare more deadly than marijuana was now laid for his unwary feet.

The new train of events began, as had the former one, at the El Paso Cafe. After drinking there for a while one day with three other men, Luis accompanied his companions to a second beer joint to enjoy a fresh round of beverages. It was there that the foursome was joined by a man named Ernesto, whom Luis had never met before. Like José, he had a role to play in the Enemy's unfolding scheme.

It was close to midnight when Ernesto made a suggestion that was to have far-reaching consequences.

"Let's go to Mexico," Ernesto abruptly proposed.

"Let's go!" Luis replied with enthusiasm. But by this time Luis was drunk.

The other men declined to accompany them, but the idea of a trip across the border rapidly became a fixation for Luis and Ernesto. Unsteadily they made their way out of the café to Luis's car, where Luis — in no condition to drive — got behind the wheel.

The trip proceeded without event until they had passed through Waco and were just on the other side of Temple, which was some 35 miles down the road. Ernesto was by this time unconscious in the front seat opposite Luis. Luis himself was struggling against extreme drowsiness. He had not been out on the open road in such a state of intoxication as this since that time, some four years before, when he had been followed by the enigmatic Thunderbird. But tonight, on a highway made slick by rain, there was no Thunderbird in sight.

Sleep now closed in on Luis. The Le Mans veered sharply off the slippery road and onto the soggy ground of an adjoining field. Something in the motion of the car suddenly jerked Luis awake.

Instinctively he realized that the vehicle was bogging down in the rain-soaked soil beneath its wheels. In what was little more than a reflex action, Luis hit the gas and gunned the car forward, guiding it through a series of ragged twists and turns until somehow he got it back onto the highway again.

Shaken by the experience, Luis cut off the motor and sat for several minutes trying to compose himself. Ernesto had remained beside him in oblivion. But when Luis glanced out into the field from which he had just come, his heart leaped to his throat.

There were trees out in that field — about a half-dozen of them. He did not even remember seeing them while he was maneuvering the car. How he had managed to avoid them completely he could not even begin to guess.

Luis's mind was still too clouded by beer to realize how close he had come to sharing Bobby's fate. Nor did he pause to compare this experience with the Thunderbird incident of years before. Yet clearly, another Hand beside his own had been on his steering wheel this night.

Ernesto was now awake, but blissfully unaware of how easily he might have awakened in another world.

"We gotta find a place to pull off," Luis informed him firmly. "I'm too drunk to drive and you're too drunk to drive. I've gotta get some sleep."

At the moment Ernesto had neither the wit nor the will to protest. After a drive of only two or three miles they came to a roadside park. There Luis pulled in and slept away the remainder of that harrowing night.

In the morning the brakes were bad and Luis stopped at a garage in Georgetown. The man there suggested that he drive on to Austin to a Pontiac dealership and take advantage of his warranty. Luis decided to do that, not guessing that his trip would end in that city as the Enemy's noose tightened.

At the Pontiac place he encountered problems.

"We'll have it for you first thing Monday morning," the garage man assured him. It was now about the middle of the day on Saturday.

"Hey, I can't wait that long," Luis objected. "I'm on vacation and there ain't nothing to do here in Austin. I've got to get out of here today."

"I'm sorry," the man replied, "but we close in a couple of hours. I can't get it for you today."

"Listen," Luis warned him, "if you don't fix it for me now, I'm going to call the Pontiac company and tell them you wouldn't help me while I was on vacation. I need my car *today!*"

The man gave a slight shrug of resignation, thus joining the long list of individuals who had collided with Luis's intransigent nature. By 3 o'clock that afternoon the car had been repaired and was ready to go.

But it didn't go to Mexico. Somehow that trip now seemed less important than finding a place to drink. It would soon be evening, and after all, what was Saturday night all about, anyway? Luis and Ernesto soon found themselves in an Austin beer joint.

When they visited a second café, they were joined by two other Hispanic men named Renaldo and Albert. After drinking heartily for some time, Ernesto was ready for a change of pace.

"Hey, anybody got a couple of joints?" he asked.

"Not me, man," Albert responded.

"Me either," Renaldo countered. "But I think I know where you can buy some."

"Let's go there," Ernesto urged eagerly.

The four of them set out in the Le Mans for the house in question. Renaldo went in and bought two joints of marijuana with Ernesto's money and brought them out to him. As they drove away, Ernesto lit one up but failed to pass it around. After a while this aroused the ire of his companions.

"Say, this dude's not sharing his joint," Albert remarked in an offended tone of voice.

"Yeah. That's not right," Luis and Renaldo agreed. "He's too greedy."

"Okay, okay, man!" Ernesto gave way. "Here's the other joint. You all light that one up."

They did so and passed it around so that everyone got a few puffs. When their marijuana was pretty well exhausted they headed for another drinking place where there would also be some dancing. Here the foursome came to blows.

Luis was well-stocked with cash. He was carrying money for a car payment which he had failed to make on Friday afternoon. Generously he ordered the first round of beers at their new location. Albert in particular had made a point of not having any money. The change from the ten dollar bill he had handed the waitress was still on the table when Luis went briefly to a restroom. When he got back it was gone, but Albert had bought cigarettes and was putting coins in a jukebox.

"I thought he said he didn't have no money," Luis observed to Renaldo. "He took my change, didn't he?"

"Yeah, he probably did," replied Renaldo, trying to make it sound like he had not observed the actual theft.

Luis managed to suppress his indignation for the moment, though usually his temper was easy to trigger after only a few beers. Meanwhile Ernesto had said or done something that was embroiling him in a controversy of his own with another patron in the café. Observing this, Renaldo turned to Luis.

"Tell you what, Luis," he began. "You take my friend outside and I'll take your friend outside and we'll put a beating on them. They're so stoned they ought to be whipped. Maybe it'll knock some sense into their heads."

Luis didn't need to be asked twice. He and Renaldo corralled each other's buddies and hustled them outside. While Renaldo scuffled ineffectually with Ernesto, Luis took aim at Albert and landed a hard punch to his face which staggered him backward.

"Hey, man," Albert protested, "what'd you jump on me for?"

"You got my money, man," Luis charged.

"I didn't get your money," Albert insisted, summoning up a tone of injured innocence.

"You know cotton-picking well you got my money," Luis rejoined sharply. "A few minutes ago you didn't have no money and here you show up with some. Where'd you get it? You think I don't know? I ought to jump on you again and beat the ____ out of you!"

"Awright, awright," Albert backed down, "so I got your money. I'm sorry about that, man. I'll let you have back what I didn't spend, okay?"

Just at that moment Renaldo, whose brief scuffle with Ernesto had ended, came up and landed a fresh punch on his startled friend. But with that the fracas was over. Beer brawls, like sudden summer squalls, often dissipated as swiftly as they arose. Within minutes, the foursome was inside the café again, drinking together as if nothing unusual had happened.

But the fight had raised the level of excitement and made the beer seem a trifle tame. What else could the evening offer as an encore to an event which had gotten everyone's adrenalin vigorously pumping? Renaldo had an idea.

"I'm going to go get me some hard stuff," he announced.

"I don't like that stuff," Luis interjected.

"Well, I'm going to go shoot me some," Renaldo continued.

"Oh, I thought you were talking about liquor," Luis reacted with surprise. Luis had never liked hard liquor, but Renaldo wasn't talking about that.

"Naw, man," Renaldo advised him, "I'm going to go shoot some H."

Heroin! Luis had never touched the drug before. The chances were good that if sober he would not have touched it now. But by this time Luis was scarcely sober.

"All right," he agreed, accepting the implied invitation, "let's go get it!"

As the Le Mans drove off with its four occupants, Luis's supernatural Adversary might well have smiled malevolently. If he could hook Luis as thoroughly on heroin as he was evidently hooked on beer, it could prove to be his most effective stratagem so far. Nothing that the divine Hand had thus far done to remake Luis's lifestyle was likely to survive an addiction like that. Along that road lay misery, ruin, and finally death — perhaps even a death beside which the tragedy of Bobby's end would pale by comparison.

Renaldo directed them to the place he had in mind, a house situated in an Austin barrio. While the others waited for him in the car, he went inside to make the purchase with money furnished by Luis. When he emerged again, he carried a small cellophane package containing a white, powdery substance.

The next step was to find a means of injecting it. Renaldo knew someone who owned a homemade needle and proceeded to direct them there. Inside the foursome prepared to shoot up.

The beer had driven every vestige of caution from Luis's mind. Homemade needles were especially hazardous. There was not only the danger of transmitted disease but also the possibility that a bubble of air might be injected into the veins along with the heroin, an occurrence which could prove fatal. Besides that, if the heroin were insufficiently broken up before shooting it into the bloodstream, a lump could travel directly to the heart and could kill.

The needle was now passed from one to the other until all four had taken injections. Within minutes Luis was sky-high. An incredible feeling of euphoria possessed him and an overwhelming sense that he could do nothing wrong.

What a lie *that* was! For at the moment he could do nothing right. Yet this was the manner in which heroin caused reality to be swallowed up by unreality, and truth by falsehood. The world into which Luis had just stepped was an illusion. But it was an illusion so powerful that many thousands of people had come to the point where it was the only world they wanted.

That was the first time they shot their narcotic that night. Later, when the effects of the initial dose had worn off, they came back to the man with the needle and injected the remainder of their purchase. Well after midnight, Luis pulled the Le Mans into an alley, where all four slept soundly until sometime around 10 or 11 the next morning.

The activities of Sunday were scarcely distinguishable from those of Saturday. After getting a bite to eat, they went back to drinking as soon as the beer joints were open. And once again the subject of heroin was raised.

"Want to go get some more H?" Renaldo asked.

"Yeah," Luis agreed, "let's go get it." He had liked the experience of the night before and he still had adequate cash to finance another round.

The Le Mans sped off again to the house where the fresh supply of "horse" could be bought and then to the other residence to use the needle. Before the day had ended, twice more they injected the drug and passed through the gates of illusion to which it granted them access.

That night Luis and Ernesto slept in the car in front of Renaldo's home. When Monday morning arrived the two of them went for breakfast and returned to bid their friend farewell. Without Renaldo's guidance into the illicit pleasures of the past weekend, Austin might have proved intolerably dull.

But it was time to get home, Luis decided. Feliz would have no idea where he was, and he had really been scheduled to work at the bakery on Sunday as well as today. Besides, his money was running out!

Before long the Le Mans was making good time up the highway back to Dallas. Austin and the experiences it had furnished receded rapidly into the distance behind them. Had he chosen to do it, Luis might have weighed the significance of the weekend's events and wondered about their impact on his future. But as usual he did not. He was going home, and just now that was all that mattered.

Of course, he *was* going home. But the question he neither asked nor answered ought to have been, *To what?*

16
A House Divided

When Luis got back to Dallas, he did something unusual. After dropping Ernesto off in Oak Cliff, he headed straight for Zane's house, in the north part of town. He did not even bother to stop by his own place, on La Salle. But even if he had, he would have found no one there.

It was the middle of the afternoon when he arrived, and Zane was home.

"I just got back from Austin," he told him. "I've got to get some sleep." The fact was that Luis felt exhausted from his profligate weekend.

"Okay," Zane agreed, "but don't you think you ought to call your family? They've been worried about you all weekend and they called over here to see if I had seen you."

"I'll call them later," Luis replied. "Right now I've gotta sack out."

Luis lay down on a couch and swiftly drifted into slumber. Meanwhile Zane phoned Luis's parents, with whom Feliz and the boys had spent an anxious weekend. Pretty soon she and Luis and Julia Rodriguez arrived at the house. Awakening the sleeping prodigal, they confronted him angrily.

"Where have you been?" Julia demanded indignantly.

"I've been gone," was Luis's curt response.

"We know *that,*" his mother retorted. "We've been looking everywhere for you. We even called the police and the highway patrol."

The memory of that was painful to Feliz as she stood by silently, listening to this exchange. The police had indeed been called and had sent an officer to the Rodriguez residence. But he had refused to take a missing persons report, dismissing the problem with the uncaring words, "He's probably just got another woman." It had hurt Feliz to think that this might be so.

"You don't have to worry about *me,*" Luis rejoined. There was a note of belligerence in that. Translated, it meant, "Why don't you stay out of my business!"

"Listen, boy," Julia lectured him, "you've got a family now and a lot of responsibilities, and here you are running around worrying everybody, and nobody knowing where you are, and the highway patrol out looking for you, and everything else. It's about time you got some sense through your head."

"He's nothing but a _____ bum," Luis's father interjected. "That's what he's always been and that's what he'll always be. He don't deserve no wife and family."

Luis listened to this tirade in silence. Once his parents got started like that, any rebuttal from him was like pouring gasoline on a fire. He had once defused such a joint assault by feigning a desire to commit suicide, but he was in no mood for that right now. The events in Austin were themselves beginning to bear a terrifying resemblance to an attempt at self-destruction.

The argument ended with no satisfactory resolution. Feliz and his parents left, while Luis remained at Zane's house. That evening, just before he also left, Luis shattered his friend's composure with an unwanted revelation.

"Zane, I'm on drugs," he suddenly blurted out. There was a tone of anguish in his voice that Zane had never heard before.

"You're on *what?*" was the startled reply.

"I'm on drugs. I'm taking heroin."

A sick feeling of horror crept over the preacher. If Luis was becoming addicted to heroin, from a human point of view the prognosis was grim. Only a tiny percentage of such addicts ever escaped the trap into which they had fallen.

"How did you get involved with *that?*" his friend asked, obviously upset.

Luis explained in very general terms. "I got down there in Austin and started fooling around with some guys, and one thing led to another, and pretty soon we were shooting heroin."

"Luis," Zane admonished him vigorously, "you'll ruin yourself if you keep doing that! Heroin will destroy you! You have to get off of it completely!"

"I need a couple of days to dry out," Luis suggested. "I want to get this stuff out of me. I need someone to watch me and not let me start back. I think I know where I can go, too." Then, with a note of resolve, he added, "I know I can kick it."

Neither Luis nor Zane realized at the time that there was as yet no real addiction. Thus a period of withdrawal was not actually needed. What was needed was determination on Luis's part to have nothing further to do with drugs.

Before he drove off that night, Luis heard another of Zane's minisermons on the kind of lifestyle a Christian ought to have. It was nothing new. Over the years Luis had been subjected to more than a little private preaching by this man. As a rule he endured it stoically, then consigned it at once to forgetfulness and to neglect.

Luis took up residence in the home of a black friend named Sonny. Sonny lived with his mother, Geneva, in far South Dallas. It was the closest thing the city had to a ghetto, though it fell well short of achieving the notoriety of places like Harlem or Watts.

Luis had first met Sonny during the days not too far past, when Sonny had lived in Oak Cliff. Their first encounter had taken place in front of the home of Luis's mother-in-law, where Luis and a half-brother of Feliz named Victor had been working on a car. Sonny had simply walked up and begun to talk. On a subsequent occasion, when Luis and Victor were doing the same thing, he had stopped to chat again. He was a friendly sort — that much was clear — and Luis liked him.

There was no real prejudice in Luis. Hispanics had experienced more than their share of discrimination and could empathize with the black experience. After a while Sonny began to stop over at Luis's apartment on La Salle to drink with him and shoot the breeze. Rather quickly they became friends. So when Luis showed up at the home of Sonny's mother in need of a place to stay, he was welcomed there with cordial hospitality. Geneva also liked her son's Latino friend.

Luis didn't try to go to work that Tuesday. He was not in the mood. Furthermore, he suspected that his days at the bakery were over. And in this respect he was not mistaken.

When he got there Wednesday morning his time card had already been pulled. This necessitated a visit to the manager's office, which had already been the scene of more than one disagreeable encounter.

"Where have you been the last three days?" the manager demanded unpleasantly.

"I didn't come in," Luis replied, as though telling him something he didn't already know.

"Yeah. Do you have a doctor's excuse?"

"No."

"In that case, you're fired," the man informed him. "You can pick your check up tomorrow."

After leaving the office, Luis encountered the union steward.

"Hey, listen," the steward told him, "we'll send you to a doctor who helps us out a lot. He'll write you up an excuse and they'll have to keep you."

"Sounds good to me," Luis responded in apparent agreement.

But he didn't bother to see the doctor. He was tired of the bakery by now and realized that more than ever he would be disliked by his boss even if the man were required to revoke the dismissal. So why fight it? It was time to quit.

When he returned on Thursday for his check, the manager had evidently heard that he might bring clearance from a physician.

"Well," he asked, "do you have a doctor's excuse?"

"No," Luis replied in a rerun of the day before.

"In that case, you're fired," the man announced once more.

"You can't fire me," Luis retorted. "I quit last Friday." No use giving him the satisfaction of winning the final round, Luis decided.

"Well, whatever," the manager replied coldly. "Just get out of here, that's all."

"Give me my check and I'll leave," Luis told him, and with that in his hand he abandoned this prickly verbal arena for good. He now had more than his share of such arenas anyway, and his recent escapades had escalated the vocal sparring in all of them.

The family situation was especially bad and could only be aggravated by his loss of employment. Feliz and his two sons continued to live with Luis's parents. After a week or so, he and Feliz decided to try and talk. For this purpose they drove to Kiest Park in the Le Mans and pulled in at a picnic area. There, both in the car and sitting on a picnic bench, they engaged in a long and fruitless discussion.

"We're not going to be able to make it work if you don't change," Feliz told him.

"Yeah, I need to change," Luis conceded.

"You've got to get a job and stop drinking and start bringing your check home and taking care of the family," she said, pursuing her theme.

"Yeah."

"What are you going to do about the car?" Feliz wanted to know. Things seemed to have soured ever since Luis purchased the Le Mans.

"I'm going to keep it," Luis told her.

"You're already a payment behind and there'll be another one pretty soon. How are you going to keep it without any job?"

"I don't know. I'll find a way," Luis replied, digging in on the issue stubbornly.

"You ought to let it go back," Feliz insisted. "Ever since you got it, it's gone to your head. It's best to let it go back."

"I'm still going to keep it. I've gotta have my wheels."

"But you'll just be running around in it like you've always done. Things won't be any different. You'll just take off some other weekend like you did the weekend before last. It won't work this way, Luis."

"Maybe not, if you say it won't," Luis shrugged with no hint of relenting.

"How are you going to pay for it? My check's not enough for that and for everything else we need, too."

"I don't know, Fel. I just want to keep it, that's all."

The conversation dragged on as the young couple went round and round on the same subjects many times. Instead of resolving their conflicts, they succeeded only in rubbing the wounds in their relationship raw. When they finally drove away from the park, they both knew that their separation would continue. Whether the marriage could be salvaged at all was in serious doubt.

Luis, however, was soon working again. Sonny got him on at his own place of employment, a mattress factory called Regal Sleep.

One day Luis went over to his parents' home, hoping to spend some time with his boys. There he encountered the fury of his father.

"What are you doing here?" the senior Luis demanded to know. "If you don't want to provide for your own family, I don't want to see you around this house! So get your ____ out of here right now!"

Luis swiftly withdrew and didn't try to come back. It was not his style to go where he was not wanted. But he still missed Viviano and Raul. Though he would not admit it, he also missed Feliz.

For a while Luis ran around a little with Sonny. Sonny drank, but neither he nor his friends were into drugs. Luis had made up his mind that narcotics were a scene he wanted no part of anymore. But the black bars of South Dallas were another matter. In time Luis knew his way around these pretty well and had made quite a few acquaintances.

One evening he strolled into a café called Robert's Place and saw a cousin of Sonny's named Leo sitting at the bar. Leo was a huge six-foot-plus hulk of a figure and was held in considerable awe by everyone who knew him. Luis approached Leo from behind.

"Hey, nigger!" he called out belligerently. "You're in my chair!"

His bravado electrified the café. People looked up from their drinks with startled expressions, fully expecting Leo to mop up the floor with this reckless Latino. "That Mexican's fixin' to get his," was the obvious general consensus.

Leo remained seated, seemingly ignoring the newcomer, while the audience watched them tensely.

"I don't know whether you heard me or not, nigger," Luis renewed his challenge, "but I said you were in my chair and I want you out of it!"

Leo now broke his stolid silence. "I'm going to get up out of this chair, man, but when I do you better not be there!"

With that threat Leo rose ominously from his seat. As he did so, Luis slipped into it.

"Get out of my chair, Mexican!" Leo chided with the faintest trace of a smile.

"It's *my* chair now," Luis shot back triumphantly.

Leo turned to the bartender. "Bring this Mexican a beer, will you? He ain't got a lick of sense! Been like that ever since I've known him!"

The words were spoken in jest, but they might equally have been said in all seriousness. Good sense was not the benchmark for Luis's way of life, and quite slowly he was becoming painfully sensitive to that fact. The separation from his family had really begun to hurt.

Geneva treated him like a second son and seemed only too happy to cook for him. Her first efforts were soul food, which Luis didn't care for but gamely tried to eat. Geneva noticed this.

"You don't like this kind of food, do you, baby?" Geneva loved to refer to Luis as her "baby."

"It's okay, Geneva," Luis tried to assure her, "I'm just not used to it, that's all."

"That's all right, baby," Geneva intoned. "You don't have to eat it. I'll get you something else."

Thereafter Geneva began to buy Mexican food in the form of TV dinners. Since these contained onions, Luis was worse off than before. Still, he didn't want to offend her, so he did his best to consume them.

One day at dinner Sonny spoke up. He had been miffed for some time at the special treatment Luis received from Geneva.

"Luis don't like those dinners," he informed his mother. "They got onions in them and Luis don't like onions."

"Oh, is that so?" Geneva was surprised. "I didn't know my baby don't like no onions."

"How come you always fix something special for Luis?" Sonny continued grumpily.

"Don't you worry 'bout that," she rejoined with motherly sternness. "He don't like our food and he needs to eat right. Don't you worry 'bout what I fix for Luis."

"Hey, that's all right," Luis intervened. "You don't need to do nothing special for me, Geneva. I'll just eat what you all eat. It'll be okay." *It'll sure be better than these onions,* he was thinking to himself.

The TV dinners stopped, but not Geneva's efforts to please her guest. Jalepeño peppers, cans of tamales, and other Mexican food items now became a regular part of the fare she served up to him. Luis appreciated her kindness, but it was still no substitute for a meal at home. As a cook, Feliz had come a long way since her initial efforts at fixing macaroni. Luis often fondly savored the memory of dinner with his own wife and children.

At nights Luis was now much less inclined to go out drinking with Sonny than he had been at first. When supper was over he might watch a little TV, then retire to the room he shared with Sonny to read his Bible. It was a remarkable step for Luis to take, something he had hardly ever done by himself since those days at Gatesville so long ago. But it irked Sonny to be deprived of such a good drinking buddy.

"C'mon, Luis," Sonny would often cajole him, "let's go have a few beers."

"Naw, I don't want to go," Luis usually replied. "I'm going to stay in tonight."

"Aw, c'mon, man," Sonny might wheedle. "We'll go pick up Leo and check out Robert's Place. I need a few cold ones."

"If you want to go, Sonny, go ahead," Luis would tell him. "Take the car if you want to. I'll stay here with Geneva and Brenda." Brenda was Sonny's sister.

One evening while Sonny was doing his best to coax Luis into going out, Geneva walked into the bedroom where they were sitting. Luis had his Bible out and had been trying to read.

"Why don't you leave Luis alone, Sonny?" Geneva remonstrated. "Can't you see he's trying to get back to God and do right? Don't you know he's got a wife and kids to think about? Just let him be. He's got enough on his mind without you jabbering away at him all the time!"

Chastened by this rebuke, Sonny rose and went out. So did Geneva, and Luis was left along with his Bible and with God.

It was a strange fact of Luis's experience that at just those times when he most missed the warmth of his loved ones, he found compassion from some other quarter. At Gatesville there had been Mr. Smith's considerate regard and help. Here it was Geneva's. And behind it all there was his heavenly Father's. Luis in fact had every reason to concur with the Apostle Paul's profound persuasion that "neither death nor life nor angels nor principalities nor powers" would be able to separate him from the love of God which he had found in Jesus Christ his Lord.

Alone and saddened by the rupture of his marriage, it was to that supernatural love that Luis turned now. Though his limited schooling made reading the Bible a difficult chore, Luis struggled to understand as much as he could of what he read each day. In addition to this, he prayed.

"Father," he requested more than once, "help the family to get back together again. Help me to stop doing the things that have caused so much trouble."

It could not be said, however, that Luis prayed this prayer with a great deal of faith. It was hard for him to believe that he was entitled to the kind of help he was asking for. It was easier to feel that his troubles were deserved, as indeed they were, and he often told himself that he had made a hopeless mess of things. As a result, he started talking seriously to Sonny about the possibility of moving to California. Perhaps there he could forget everything that had happened and start over.

It was October now, and the State Fair of Texas was once again in full swing. It would have been painful for Luis to remember that one of his first dates with Feliz had been at the fair, where his friend Arnulfo had contrived for them to meet. But this year he at least wanted to take his boys one night, and so he phoned his parents' house to ask one of his sisters to bring them. Since his banishment from the parental residence had not been lifted — or so he chose to believe — he could not go by for them but would wait at a prearranged spot on the fairgrounds.

When the boys arrived, however, it was not a sister who was with them, but Feliz.

"Hi, Fel," Luis greeted her, hiding his surprise.

Feliz responded with a tense but friendly smile.

"How are you?" Luis asked.

"I'm fine. How are you?"

"I'm okay too," he replied.

With the boys in tow, Luis and Feliz made their way through the crowd that thronged the Midway. They engaged in small talk and filled each other in on all the pertinent news. But about the problems that had divided their household they said nothing at all.

When the evening was over they once again went their separate ways. Luis hugged Viviano and Raul and bid them all goodbye.

"So long, Feliz. I'll see you around."

"You be careful, Luis. Goodbye."

Not long after this encounter, Luis bought a record and sent it to his parents' house for Feliz. On one side was a touching song called "So Long, My Love," in which the vocalist lamented his irreparable parting from the object of his affections. It was a simple but telling gesture for Luis to make. In a way too subtle to describe, for the Latino music was truly the language of the heart.

In the meanwhile Mrs. Rodriguez contacted Luis, asking for money to defray the expense of caring for his sons. She complained that Feliz spent most of her salary on clothes and contributed little to the cost of feeding them. Luis sent some, but his mother continued to express unhappiness at her burdens and managed to make Feliz increasingly uncomfortable by doing so.

In reality, Julia had observed that Feliz now frequently went to weekend dances with her sisters-in-law and stayed out late. She correctly assessed this as a dangerous trend. The pressures she exerted about monetary matters in retrospect looked like a subtle way of hastening a reconciliation. But she was far too shrewd to suggest this directly.

One day the phone rang at Geneva's. It was Feliz calling for Luis.

"Is that you, Fel?" Luis asked when he got to the phone.

"Yes, it is. I just wanted to know what your plans were. Did you get your apartment yet?" At the fair he had told her he wanted to move into his own apartment. Though he paid Geneva a weekly rent, he felt he had burdened her long enough. He was anxious to be on his own.

"No, not yet," Luis replied. "Maybe pretty soon."

"Do you think you could get an apartment big enough for all four of us?" she suggested cautiously.

"I don't know about that. I don't think I have enough money for one that big." At Regal Sleep he made quite a bit less than he had made at the unionized A & P.

"Well, I'm still working," Feliz reminded him. "My check would help."

"If we're going to try to go back together, we ought to go back to La Salle. All our stuff is over there and we're only one payment behind."

The young couple had been buying their half of the duplex. Their separation had not yet been long enough for them to lose it. The items of furniture they owned still sat in the vacant apartment like silent sentries awaiting their owners' return. The vigil, if such it could be called, was now about to end.

"All right," said Feliz, "let's try it again."

17
At the Foot of the Stairs

Years before, on the morning of his release from Gatesville, Luis had descended the dormitory stairway only to encounter his enemies Joaquin, Sergio, and Oscar. For a few tense moments his future hung in the balance at the foot of those stairs.

And so it was now. Once again Luis stood at the foot of the stairs. The reunion with his family could have either of two opposite results. It could either solidify his marriage, or lead to its complete collapse. If the marriage collapsed, the whole course of Luis's life would be changed. The prospect of that carried the promise of tragedy.

The family was once again living in their La Salle Street home. Like so many wives before her, Feliz hoped for a miraculous transformation in her husband. But she was soon disappointed. Relieved of the anxieties created by their separation, Luis settled back into his normal ways. The drinking companion whom Sonny thought he had lost was found again.

More than once Feliz threatened to leave. Luis gave her plenty of reasons to do so. One night when Luis had been drinking heavily, he threatened her with a kitchen knife. Feliz ran out of the house and down the street in the direction of her mother's place. But Luis ran after her and persuaded her to come back.

There were other tensions. Luis got involved again with stealing. What he had tried to avoid at the A & P he tolerated at Regal Sleep, where he now drove a truck. When the shipping clerk asked Luis to deliver a box spring and mattress to the clerk's apartment, Luis agreed to do it. But he knew it was a rip-off of company goods.

The house on La Salle Street was the point of rendezvous for a similar theft. That day Feliz watched with dismay as two or three mattresses were transferred from the company truck to a pickup truck driven by two of the shipping clerk's friends.

"How come you brought those mattresses over here?" she asked with obvious suspicion.

"So those guys could pick them up," Luis told her.

"Are they stolen?"

"Naw, they're not stolen," Luis lied.

Feliz thought otherwise. "I don't want you bringing them over here," she said firmly. "If they're stolen, I don't want them coming over here."

Luis knew she was right. There were no more transfers of stolen mattresses at their La Salle Street home. But that may have been due much less to a feeling for integrity than to a decisive incident that took place soon after at Regal Sleep.

A new manager had recently come on the job there. One day he found Luis upstairs at the warehouse helping his fellow workers with a chore. That was where Luis generally worked when he wasn't on his route.

"Luis!" the manager ordered him sharply. "You go downstairs and bag those mattresses down there."

It wasn't a very considerate request. Bagging mattresses was a task for more than one man, and no one else was downstairs at the moment. Typically, Luis's temper flared.

"What's the matter with you?" he shot back indignantly. "Are you stupid or just plain dumb? You know just one person can't bag mattresses! If you don't know that, I don't know what you're doing here!"

The manager glared at him for a few seconds. Then he

turned and stalked out. About 15 minutes later he met Luis downstairs.

"Here," said the manager thrusting a check into Luis's hand. "This is your money. You don't have a job here anymore."

It was like the rerun of a bad movie. Losing jobs needlessly was a perverse talent that Luis needed to bury and forget. Yet surprisingly, he quickly found work again. Within a few days he was driving a truck for a paper goods place called Artex Lane.

The transition proved to be yet another unmerited kindness bestowed by an unseen Hand. The circumstances at Artex Lane were far superior to those at Regal Sleep. Here there was no systematic stealing, and Luis's fellow workers were more inclined to go home at night than they were to go out and drink.

Luis himself headed home on a more regular basis. The amount of his weekly check which was consumed on beer dropped off sharply. His time at this new place of employment slowly lengthened toward the two-year mark.

Subtle changes were now taking place which even Feliz began to notice. Viviano was about five years old and loved to help his dad work on his car. About all he was able to do was to hand his father the tools and get himself horribly greasy, but somehow this touched Luis. Gradually Luis began to sense his boys' need for a more positive fatherly image. Who else was going to teach them how to handle a bat or toss a football?

To bring more cash into the family coffers, Luis sometimes spent Sunday morning cleaning up the office area at Artex Lane. This activity became a family event when Feliz and the boys began to accompany him. While the parents worked, Viviano and Raul played their hearts out, whooping and hollering with delight as they ran around the paper goods warehouse. It was a small thing, but it added a little cohesion to the family's experience.

Somewhat more often now, the family went to Luis's church. Many pleasant childhood memories clung to this church in Luis's mind, and increasingly he wanted his own children to be there. Feliz was only too happy for her husband to go and was ready to attend with him whenever he suggested it.

Still, she squirmed a bit while she listened to the sermons, and she found it increasingly difficult to cope with the appeals to "get saved."

Luis frequently passed by Zane's house as he was on his way to or from his delivery route. Often this was only for a brief, inconsequential chat. But at other times, when he got off from work, there were Bible studies. They even ate a meal together on several occasions to observe the Lord's Supper.

Nevertheless the old lifestyle clung to Luis like a bloodsucking leech. If his fellow workers at Artex Lane did not drink a whole lot, they still drank. Luis frequently joined a couple of them at a beer joint not far from the job.

But instead of drinking until midnight and beyond, as he had so often done at the El Paso Cafe, he and his companions usually quit about 8 o'clock and headed home. It was no doubt an improvement, though an exceedingly modest one.

The owner of the café treated Luis as a valued and trusted customer. Luis was allowed to run his credit up as high as 30 dollars. At 50 cents a drink, that represented quite a few beers. One day Luis was talking to the man about his bill.

"Listen," he told him, "I'm having a little problem getting money to pay you." Family expenses now had a high priority for Luis.

"That's okay," the owner replied generously, "I know you're good for it. You'll pay me when you can."

"I just didn't want you to think I wasn't going to pay up," Luis continued, trying to underscore his good intentions.

"Yeah, like I said, it's okay."

There was a pause and then the proprietor spoke up again as if a new thought had just struck him. It was an idea whose Source Luis ought to have recognized by now.

"Say," the man asked, "over there at your work, do you have some paper bags that a six-pack would go into?"

"Yeah, we've got lots of them."

"Tell you what I'll do," the owner proposed. "Why don't you get me 500 of those bags. They're probably worth about 10 cents apiece, and I could take 20 bucks off your bill and you could just give me a ten. That way we'll both come out ahead. What do you think?"

"Sounds good to me," Luis agreed. "I'll see what I can do."

It was wrong, of course. Luis knew that. But it was an easy way to reduce his bill without biting into the family budget. One day shortly afterward, when his supervisor was not watching, Luis pulled the 500 bags from the warehouse and loaded them into his truck. He delivered them to the proprietor of the café and received the promised credit.

His Enemy was still a master of manipulation.

Sorrow again entered Luis's life. One morning his phone rang at 6 A.M. It was his mother and her news was somber.

"Dad just died," she reported in a subdued tone of voice.

"What did he die of?" Luis asked. The information shocked him.

"We don't know yet. He passed away while they were taking him to the hospital," Julia replied. She sounded remarkably composed, and for the moment she was.

It turned out that the senior Luis had developed trouble in breathing early that morning. An ambulance had been summoned and had raced away from the Rodriguez residence with its siren blaring. But as it approached Stemmons Expressway, which it would take all the way to Parkland Hospital, the siren was abruptly cut off. Luis's father had passed into eternity.

Luis took a week's vacation time from Artex Lane in order to be with his grieving family. This was a substantial loss which Luis genuinely felt, despite the friction he had often experienced with his dad. But it did not leave Luis fatherless. What his human father had failed to accomplish in his son, his other Father still worked to achieve. And He did this with a superb patience which the earthly parent had never been able to command.

But Luis seemed determined to test that patience to the uttermost. Not long after his father's death, Luis changed jobs. At the urging of his old buddy Cecil, in whose home he and Feliz had been married, Luis went to work at a place called Superior Circuits. The company made circuit boards for the government and private businesses. On his new job Luis could earn 15 or 20 cents more per hour than at Artex Lane.

The shift to Superior Circuits had undesirable results. Cecil liked to stay out late and drink, and Luis naturally joined him in this. It was not unusual for Luis to consume two or three evenings a week in a beer joint until it was closing time. Predictably this raised tensions at home in his marriage.

But somehow the decline was not as steep as before. Luis continued to feel the tug which his sons now exercised on his heart. His years of spasmodic exposure to the Bible had created a kind of cumulative impact on his consciousness which was becoming more and more difficult for him to ignore. In ways which he himself would have found difficult to express, he had begun to despise his old lifestyle and all that went with it. It was like the cinnamon rolls his father had once compelled him to eat in such excessive quantity that he never wanted any more. Luis was almost surfeited with sin.

One day at Superior Circuits, Luis dropped in on a noon-hour Bible study which was being conducted by a young seminary graduate named John Comfort. As it happened, the discussion focused on a statement found in the Gospel of John in which Jesus offered eternal life to anyone who would believe Him for it. The statement might well have been His most famous one: "For God so loved the world that He gave His only begotten Son, so that whoever believes in Him should not perish but have everlasting life."

John Comfort was prodding his audience to express what they thought it meant to be a Christian. A young woman in the group spoke up emphatically.

"A lot of people claim to be Christians these days and they're really not," she asserted. "The way they live shows they're not Christians at all. They may call themselves Christians, but they're just using the word. There's nothing more to it than that."

This statement was more than Luis could sit still for. He decided to enter the discussion.

"Well, *I'm* a Christian," he informed the group and the female speaker in particular.

The girl looked at him with an incredulous stare.

"How can *you* be a Christian?" The question carried a hint of scorn. "I've seen *you* drinking in bars. Where do you get off saying *you're* a Christian?"

"But that's what this verse says," Luis pointed out. "It says that you get eternal life by believing."

"That's only the beginning," the young woman objected, "and after that you're supposed to go to church and do the right things. You can't be a Christian if you don't do that."

"No, that's not right," Luis replied, standing his ground. "That's not what salvation is. It's a free gift with no strings attached."

Naturally Luis's words reverberated with the echoes of familiar Biblical statements. One which he might have quoted said, "By grace you have been saved through faith, and this not of yourselves, it is God's gift; not of works, so that no one may boast." Luis knew what the Bible taught and he knew that he had believed.

"I have to agree with Luis," John Comfort spoke up. "Salvation is by faith alone and not by what we do. Luis is right about that."

The girl remained unconvinced, though she was staring at a man who was a living refutation of the popular notions she held. It struck her as preposterous that Luis could really be a child of God. Yet that was only because she did not understand how a person could be assured of this status by trusting the plain, uncomplicated promises of God. But Luis understood.

Happily, so very soon did Feliz. One evening she was watching a Billy Graham special on television, and the truth she had been hearing for so long suddenly became clear. Very simply, as she sat there, she opened her heart to the same gift her husband had received as a little boy.

Soon afterward she told Luis. "Luis," she said, "I got saved."

"When?" he wanted to know.

"Over at Mother's, watching Billy Graham."

"That's good, Fel. I'm glad," Luis told her.

He was, too. There was now some extra glue in a marriage that needed all it could get!

Slowly — ever so slowly — the path wound upward. By 1969 the family was attending church meetings on Sunday mornings on a regular basis. Then a small thing happened which was to have large consequences.

Horace Gill still led the singing at the church, as he had often done since its days in the clapboard building. It was Mr. Gill who had constructed the handmade wooden benches, on one of which Luis sat the night he trusted Christ. But Horace and Dorothy Gill took an annual monthlong vacation trip into the scenic regions of Colorado, and this year Luis was asked to lead the singing while they were gone.

Luis had always loved to sing, and the songs at the church were now part of the fabric of his soul. Though he experienced the usual timidity and self-consciousness, the month went surprisingly well. A few weeks after Mr. Gill returned, Luis approached him before a morning service.

"Mr. Gill, I want to retire you from song-leading," Luis informed him.

Without blinking an eye, Mr. Gill responded, "Do you want my list of songs or do you have one of your own?"

"I don't have my own list," Luis admitted.

"Well, here's mine for this morning." He handed Luis the ones he had picked out for that meeting. "Next week I'll show you something I do that may help you."

Luis led the singing that day and thereafter did it regularly. Mr. Gill showed him his own set of multiple song lists which could be used on a rotating basis. But with characteristic independence, Luis decided to make his own selections every week. Conducting a simple song service was the first continuing activity that Luis had ever undertaken for God. He found that he liked it.

It was September of 1969 when the family moved out of the La Salle Street duplex and into an apartment on Tremont Street in East Dallas. They continued to pay the mortgage on the duplex and rented it out. Luis thus became a landlord for the first time.

But there was another first at their new residence which had even greater significance. Luis's drinking had diminished greatly, and now, for the family's sake, Luis never did any drinking at home. Tremont Street was the first place the family had lived where the refrigerator was beer-can free!

When Feliz's cousins Angel and Octavio came to Dallas from Mexico the following year, Feliz had to give them special instructions.

"You can come over here and stay if you need to," she told them, "but you can't bring beer into the apartment. We don't let liquor come into our home anymore."

With liquor locked out, so were a lot of other undesirable things. The relationship between the young husband and wife grew steadily stronger.

Luis's tenure at Superior Circuits was by now the longest of any job he had ever held. He advanced from delivery man to plater, and he appeared to be in line for the position of lead man in the shop, a role just below that of foreman. Then something else transpired which was quite unprecedented.

A delivery man named Willard, whom Luis usually called "Arkansas," called regularly at Superior Circuits. He worked for a company called Continental Water and delivered the deionized-water-conditioning units which were needed for the plating operation. Luis and "Arkansas" struck up a friendship and often shot dice together. One day "Arkansas" told him about a possible job opening at Continental Water.

The opening did not materialize immediately. When Willard finally informed him that the opportunity was there, Luis was hesitant. Should he leave Superior Circuits where the prospect of advancement seemed to exist? That's when he did what he had never done before. He prayed about his job!

"Father," he requested on several consecutive nights, "show me if this is the job You want me to have. Help me to make the right decision."

Before the week was out the decision had been made. The lead man at Superior Circuits left. A former lead man named Joe, who had abruptly quit six months before, was rehired. Luis was apparently passed by in favor of someone who had forfeited his tenure. In addition, "Arkansas" came back pressing Luis for a prompt decision. Luis submitted his two-week notification.

"Why are you leaving?" the manager wanted to know.

"Well, I've been here three years," Luis explained, "and you rehired Joe after he quit and made him lead man again."

"We wish you'd stay," his boss urged him. "We'll give you 50 cents an hour more and make you lead man, too. How about it, Luis? We don't want you to leave."

"No, I don't think so," Luis replied. "I've already made my decision. But thanks anyway for the offer."

He had never left a job under better circumstances. It was nice to be wanted at two places instead of none at all! But the move to Continental Water was one he never regretted. And in the process he had learned a new lesson about the value of prayer.

At church, Luis now served as an occasional substitute teacher in a Sunday school class. Along with the song-leading, he enjoyed this as well. Eventually he took over the class on a regular basis. The church was now situated in a small but comfortable house on Llano Street. Luis's class was in one of the back rooms. He had about a dozen kids to teach, among whom were his own two sons.

Luis was far from being a polished teacher. But he related well to the everyday problems of the Latino boys and girls he taught, many of whom he knew to be Christians.

"Today," Luis might begin his lesson, "we're going to talk about how Jesus fed 5000 people at one time. He had a big crowd listening to Him one day, and it got late and they didn't have no food to eat. If they were going to get anything to eat, they'd have to go into town and buy something. That was *their* problem.

"We've got a lot of problems, too, especially if we're Christians. Take school, for instance. What kind of problems do you have there?"

With a little coaxing he could usually get the kids to respond to questions like that.

"They make fun of you," one might suggest.

"Yeah," Luis agreed. "Maybe they say, 'Hey, there goes old Christian so and so,' and they laugh at you."

"They ask why you don't use curse words," another child would observe.

"They say, 'How come you don't act up in class?' " another might offer.

"They pass around a joint and try to get you to take a puff," someone else would say.

"That's right," Luis might respond. "It gets you high, but it don't do you no good."

Then he would continue. "Okay, those are some of our problems. Let's see what Jesus did about the problem these people had. He asked his disciples what food they had there, and they didn't have nothing except five loaves and two fishes. But He took what they had and blessed it, and they gave it out to the people and everybody got enough to eat and there was still some left over.

"How about us? What do *we* have that Jesus can bless so that our problems can be solved?"

The children pondered this for a while. Luis was never quite sure what they might come up with.

"We have love," one proposed.

"Uh, yeah . . . I guess we do," Luis struggled for an application. "Maybe we can ask God to bless our love for people at school and they won't make fun of us no more."

"We have prayer," suggested another.

That was an easy one. "We sure do," Luis agreed, "and God can answer our prayers and help us with our problems." He knew about that.

"We have friendship," said another.

"What do you mean by friendship?" Luis inquired.

"Jesus is our Friend."

"Yeah . . . okay . . . that's right. Let's see . . . maybe we can ask God to make that friendship grow to other people. That could help us with the kids at school."

"We have the Bible," came the next suggestion, and so it might go on until Luis felt the point had been adequately covered.

It was too bad that Miss Williams and Miss Nichols couldn't have witnessed a scene like that! Miss Williams might very well have nudged Miss Nichols and said, "See, I told you so. I told you Luis would amount to something some day. He's coming right along, isn't he?" Miss Nichols would probably have rubbed her eyes in disbelief. Could that be the Luis she had known?

He *was* coming along. And though he never told the story in his class, Luis was experiencing the reality which lay behind an ancient Biblical narrative. Centuries ago, the prophet Elijah was standing at the entrance of a mountain cave. As he watched, in quick succession the mountain was shaken by a mighty wind, a powerful earthquake, and a devouring fire. But the Almighty was in none of these spectacular displays. Rather He was encountered in the "still, small voice" which followed them.

Such was the silent miracle which was now transpiring in Luis. More than once the fabric of his life had been torn by violence or danger or unhappy loss. But in the end it was not to these things that his heart responded, however much their lessons were needed in his life. Instead, Luis's heart was responding to the still, small voice of his heavenly Father. And that voice vibrated, as it always had, with the tones of a generous and unfailing love.

Years before, at the foot of the stairs in Gatesville, Mr. Smith had interposed himself between Luis and his enemies. His words had been, "You see that door, Luis? Hit it!" And now, as truly as it had been then, it was God who interposed Himself between Luis and his Foe. It was His gentle voice that said, "The door is there, Luis. Use it!"

There were setbacks, of course. Even during the two years in which he taught Sunday school, there were several occasions when he found himself drinking in a bar with some friend. But the inward agony that followed was worse than a hangover. His discouragement was like a piercing sword.

There's no way I can teach my class on Sunday! he might tell himself after a Friday night of beer. *A drunk don't have no business teaching the Bible!*

But that was not his Father's voice. That was his Enemy's. It was a voice he could not afford to listen to anymore.

I've got to teach my class! his heart told him emphatically. *I let the devil defeat me on Friday night, and if he keeps me from teaching my class, he'll defeat me on Sunday too! I'm not going to let him have that victory! I'm going to teach my class!*

It was about time that Luis channeled some of his notorious firmness into fulfilling the Biblical command, "Resist the devil and he will flee from you." So he taught his class that week, and he taught it in the weeks that followed, too.

And eventually there were no more Friday nights of beer.

18
The Lion's Roar

Luis stood nervously behind the pickup truck where the *Policía Federal* had left him temporarily alone. What they would decide to do with him he could not guess, but he feared the worst.

It could not be said that in those danger-filled moments Luis's life passed before his eyes. But perhaps that was just as well. Much of that life was painful to remember anyway, and there were too many things that Luis wished he could forget. But the last seven years had been different.

Luis had spent that many years with Continental Water. Viviano had turned 17 just a couple of months earlier and Raul was now 15. Both of his sons had accepted for themselves God's gift of eternal life. And they were navigating their teenage years under the tutelage of their father far better than he had done. The family was a tight-knit unit where prayer and Bible reading were a natural part of the household experience. The once-troubled home was now a happy one.

What had once been a clapboard church had graduated into a regular church structure containing a moderate sized but well-appointed auditorium. Luis was no longer a Sunday school teacher there. He was now a preacher and a pastor who shared the pulpit equally with a younger man named Stephen Hall and with Zane. When Luis preached, he could speak persuasively about the compassionate grace of his heavenly Father. And from his own experience he could warn about the deceitfulness of sin.

But at the moment it seemed possible he might never preach again. A simple squeeze of the trigger on one of those deadly machine guns could see to that.

The representatives of the *Policía Federal* were now clustered in a little knot not far from the rear of Luis's van. He was not close enough to hear what they said to each other. From sheer prudence he remained glued to the spot where they had left him.

Out of the corner of his eye he could see Angel standing somewhat to the front of the van. Octavio was close by pacing back and forth. They too were by themselves.

Eventually the group of policemen dispersed. The one who had originally ordered Luis back to the spot where he now stood headed across the highway in the direction of a man who seemed to have some authority. After a brief consultation, the policeman started back toward Luis, machine gun still at the ready.

This is it! Luis thought.

The look of hostility had in no way faded from the officer's face. His language was as vulgar as ever.

"Get the ＿＿ out of here!" He spat the words out and followed them with a string of obscenities. "You're a sorry, no good ＿＿, so get your ＿＿ out of here! We don't ever want to see you around here again, you rotten ＿＿! Do you understand?"

Luis walked slowly back to the van, escorted by this foulmouthed individual who continued to assault his ears with curses. When Luis climbed into the driver's seat, Angel and Octavio were already inside. Motioned forward by the policeman, he pulled the van back onto the highway. With due caution, he gradually left the *Policía Federal* and their roadblock behind.

"What did they want?" Octavio asked.

"I don't know," Luis replied. "They just asked a bunch of questions."

"What'd they ask?" Octavio wanted to know.

"The usual stuff, my name and things like that. I guess they were doing more cursing than asking," Luis acknowledged. "What did they ask you?"

"Same thing," Angel responded. "Our names and all that."

They were now a good hundred yards from the scene, and Octavio felt it safe to explode. His tongue was barely less acid than those of the *Policia*.

"Those sorry ____!" he fumed. "They're not worth ____! Just because they've got machine guns, they think they're mean! They're a bunch of no good ____!"

"You know," Angel interjected, "they've been known to shoot people just for the heck of it."

"That's right!" Octavio agreed. "Someday they'll be the cause of our country turning against the government. If our people ever get themselves some weapons, they'll kill those worthless ____! They have no business shooting people down. Especially you, Luis. You're just a tourist. Get a good picture of those men in your mind. Someday you'll meet one of them up there in the United States and then they'll be on *your* ground."

Luis listened to all this in silence. He could not find it in his heart to revile his enemies or to plot personal revenge on them. What he did find in his heart was a sense of gratitude.

"Father," he had prayed within minutes of leaving the roadblock, "thank You for getting us out of there."

The hours sped by until they reached Nuevo Laredo, just to the south of the Texas-Mexican border. It was late afternoon and Luis was famished.

"Let's get something to eat," he proposed to his riders.

"Who can eat?" Octavio rejoined. "I'm still thinking about those rotten ____ back there! I'm still mad as ____!"

"Octavio, you've just got to forget about that," Luis admonished him. "It doesn't do any good to stay mad."

"I know," Octavio conceded, "but I just can't get it out of my mind. I'd sure like to catch one of them someday. I'll show 'em they're not as 'bad' as they think they are!"

"Come on, Octavio," Luis chided. "They're not worth all that anger. Let's eat!"

And eat they did, in a small Nuevo Laredo café. Revitalized by this nourishment, Luis again shopped for the Choco Milk he had wanted to bring to Zane. And this time he found a can, complete with its trademark representation of the muscle-flexing Pancho Pantera. "Alimento, Vitaminado, Mineralizado" the can's exterior proclaimed proudly. Zane could use that, Luis figured.

Dropping Angel and Octavio off in the downtown area, Luis finally crossed into Laredo, on the Texas side of the border. When he did so, he breathed another prayer.

"Thank You, Lord, for getting me out of that country."

As he passed through Laredo, Luis kept his eyes open for someone he might pick up. There were often travelers in that city, frequently whole families, looking for a ride north. It would be nice to have company the rest of the way back to Dallas.

Tonight, however, there were only a few prospects to be seen along the streets. Since none of them looked particularly like the kind of company Luis wanted, he decided to pass them all by.

But what did it matter? He really was not alone. Nor had he ever been alone since the night at the clapboard church when he had put faith in the Lord Jesus Christ. He had traveled many a road since then, not a few of them perilous ones. But he had never traveled any of those roads alone.

As his Ford economy-line 250 van sped up highway 35 toward Dallas, the roadblock deep in the Mexican interior already seemed far, far away. He had heard the roar of the Lion at that roadblock. But it had not been a roar of triumph after all. Instead, it was a roar of hatred and rage, a roar of frustration and defeat.

There would be other assaults from his Enemy in the days ahead. Luis was sure of that. But what form they might take he neither tried nor cared to guess. One thing he knew. The Bible said, "Be sober, be vigilant! Your adversary the devil is walking about like a roaring lion, seeking someone whom he may devour. Resist him steadfastly in the faith."

Whenever the van crossed a hump in the highway, the can of Choco Milk would bounce a bit. But Luis and his Companion continued undisturbed on the road that was leading home.

While these pages were being written, Luis led his former drinking buddy, Sam Moon, to faith in Christ. Over a period of months, as Sam suffered from terminal cancer, Luis sat by his bed and read him the Gospel of John. Sam went home to heaven on August 16, 1981.

Good night, Sam. We'll see you in the morning!